WITTGENSTEIN: A RELIGIOUS
POINT OF VIEW?

WITTGENSTEIN: A RELIGIOUS POINT OF VIEW?

Norman Malcolm

Edited with a response by Peter Winch

Cornell University Press
Ithaca, New York

First published 1994
by Cornell University Press
Sage House, 512 East State Street
Ithaca, New York 14850
First printing, Cornell Paperbacks, 1995

Library of Congress Cataloging in Publication Data

Malcolm, Norman
Wittgenstein: a religious point of view? / Norman Malcolm
edited with a response by Peter Winch
p. cm.
Includes index
1. Wittgenstein, Ludwig 1889-1951–Religion. 2. Religious
thought–20th century. I. Winch, Peter. II. Title
B3376. W564M245   1994
210'.92–dc20   93-25808

ISBN-13: 978-0-8014-8266-3 (pbk. : alk. paper)
ISBN-10: 0-8014-8266-6 (pbk. : alk. paper)

Printed in the United States of America

Cornell University Press strives to use environmentally responsible suppliers
and materials to the fullest extent possible in the publishing of its books.
Such materials include vegetable-based, low-VOC inks and acid-free papers
that are recycled, totally chlorine-free, or partly composed of nonwood fibers.
For further information, visit our website at www.cornellpress.cornell.edu.

Paperback printing   10 9 8 7 6 5

CONTENTS

PREFACE

This essay by Norman Malcolm was the last piece of philosophical work he was able to complete before his death in the summer of 1990. The word 'complete' needs qualification. He did indeed bring the essay so far that he was willing to have it published. Indeed, he attached so much importance to the subject that I think it is correct to say that he was anxious that it should be published. At the same time, he was still working at it as far as he was able, and thinking of improvements until shortly before he died.

The subject of the essay is a remark which Wittgenstein's friend Drury quotes him as having made to him: ' I am not a religious man but I cannot help seeing every problem from a religious point of view.' [1] Norman explains his own interest in this in terms of the difficulties it raised for his own understanding and interpretation of Wittgenstein's philosophy: something that certainly stood at the very centre of his intellectual life. I never discussed Norman's religious commitments directly with him; and the present essay, like virtually all his previous published work, contains no references to his own religious beliefs or doubts. But no one who knew him at all well could have been in any doubt that religious conceptions played a pivotal role in his thinking and feeling about his life. I think, moreover, that anyone who has read his philosophical writings with perception would not be surprised to hear this. I make this point here because I think, though it is speculation, that during the last year of his life, Norman was aware that his own end was probably not far off, and that he would naturally have approached this thought in religious terms. I think too that this would have given his interest in the subject of his essay an additional dimension as he tried to take stock of his own life and the roles in it of philosophy and religion respectively. This may well have played a role in the urgency with which he tried to complete his task while he still could. But, as I said, this is speculative.

The manuscript was an awkward length from a publisher's point of view, being substantially shorter than the standard 'book'. For this reason I was asked to contribute a fairly lengthy introduction, an invitation that I accepted without hesitation, not only because of my own interest in the subject, but also in the context of the quite close friendship I was privileged to enjoy with Norman after his retirement from the Susan Linn Sage Chair of Philosophy at Cornell University and his subsequent settlement in London. This friendship was certainly much more than a merely 'professional' one, but vigorous and uninhibited philosophical discussion was a very central element in it. He was one of the very few people I have known with whom I felt that, when discussing philosophical questions, we were really addressing each other. This of course did not mean that we agreed about everything, or even about most things. On the contrary, I would say that we disagreed quite radically over many really fundamental issues. What it did mean was that each of us usually understood pretty well, and respected, what the other was saying; or that where we did not understand each other, we knew how to recognize and rectify the situation. (I think this will seem trivial only to those who have rather modest standards of what mutual understanding consists in.) A very important condition of such a relationship is of course that the parties should feel entitled, indeed obligated, to express their mutual *disagreements* as clearly and emphatically as possible.

When I came to think closely about Norman's manuscript, I found increasingly and not greatly to my surprise that my discussion of it would have to express some pretty sharp disagreements. I felt, and feel, no inhibitions about this, because of the nature of our friendship as I have sketched it. Indeed, I know that Norman would have been disgusted with anything less than an attempt at complete intellectual honesty in the discussion of his work. At the same time, it seemed to me quite inappropriate to use the format of an introduction for such a critical discussion – without first giving the poor man the chance to make his case! So I decided to split my contribution between this fairly personal explanatory preface and a discussion to *follow* Norman's essay, in which I could feel free to be as critical as I should find it necessary to be. This follows the form of one of Malcolm's own earlier publications, *Consciousness and Causality*, which he wrote in co-operation with David Armstrong.[2] My only regret is that the format cannot be completed by the hard-hitting riposte to my comments that Norman would undoubtedly have provided had he still been alive.

No apology needs to be made for publishing the essay in its present form. It is a characteristic piece of work, written with the same sturdy elegance to which his readers are long accustomed, showing no signs of lack of vigour and, it goes without saying, exuding the same unaffected intellectual honesty which was always one of the main strengths of his writing. As I have already said, though, he was still developing and revising his thoughts and would certainly have gone on doing so for a long time had he lived. During the time that I knew him well the writings that he published were the outcome, not merely of such extensive revision, but also of intensive discussion and argument with friends and students, privately and in seminars. I imagine the same was also true of what he published earlier in his life. He had no opportunity for anything like this in the case of the present essay. Had he had such an opportunity I have no doubt that he would have seen weaknesses in some of the ways in which he put his points and would have strengthened them, though I doubt whether he would have fundamentally changed his opinions. I regret very much indeed that it was not possible for me to have had such discussions with him, not least because he would certainly have been able to show me many weaknesses in my own counter-arguments. I have had to do the best I could without this help.

Peter Winch

NOTES

1 Rush Rhees (ed.), *Ludwig Wittgenstein, Personal Recollections*, Oxford, Oxford University Press, 1984, p. 94.
2 David Armstrong and Norman Malcolm, *Consciousness and Causality*, Oxford, Blackwell, 1984.

LIST OF ABBREVIATIONS

INTRODUCTION

When Wittgenstein was working on the latter part of the *Philosophical Investigations*, he said to his former student and close friend M. O'C. Drury: 'My type of thinking is not wanted in this present age; I have to swim so strongly against the tide.' In the same conversation he said: 'I am not a religious man but I cannot help seeing every problem from a religious point of view' (*R*, p. 94).

For a long time I have been puzzled by this second remark. My understanding of Wittgenstein's philosophical thought seemed to be threatened. For the 'problems' to which he was referring were not the problems of poverty, disease, unemployment, crime, brutality, racial prejudice, war. These problems oppress and bewilder mankind. Certainly they disturbed Wittgenstein. But he was not referring to them. The 'problems' he meant are *philosophical*: those very perplexities and confusions with which he grapples in the *Investigations*. Wittgenstein's remark made Drury wonder whether 'there are not dimensions in Wittgenstein's thought that are still largely being ignored', and whether he (Drury) himself understood that the problems studied in the *Investigations* 'are being seen from a religious point of view' (ibid.). I have the same doubt in regard to myself.

In this book I am going to present an interpretation of what it could mean to say that there is, *not* strictly a religious point of view, but something *analogous* to a religious point of view, in Wittgenstein's later philosophical thought. For Wittgenstein certainly did not bring religious ideas explicitly into his studies of troublesome concepts. Most students of Wittgenstein's work would be bewildered by the suggestion that he saw those problems from a

1

religious perspective. Yet his remark to Drury would seem to mean that at least Wittgenstein was aware of some point or points of analogy between his philosophical outlook and a religious one.

A possible clue may lie in the reiterated theme of his writings, that explanations, reasons, justifications, *come to an end.* This theme itself needs to be clarified. Does it mean that there are *no* explanations or justifications for anything? Or does it mean that there are – but only up to a certain point? If so, *what* is that point? Can it be described?

In religious thinking there *is* an end to explanation. To parents grieving over the death of a child, these words may be spoken: 'The Lord hath given; the Lord hath taken away. Blessed is the name of the Lord.' Not everyone will find consolation in those words. But persons of a strong religious inclination may find help there: or in the words, 'It is God's will'. This *can* quiet the cry from the heart – '*Why* did it happen?' When the search for an explanation, a reason, a justification, is brought to an end in the acknowledgement that it was God's will – that is a religious response. There is a religious attitude which would regard as meaningless, or ignorant, or presumptuous, any demand for *God's* reason or justification, or any attempt to explain why He willed, or permitted, this disaster to occur.

But even a devout man may, in his despair, murmur against God. Here the Book of Job is deeply significant. Job was 'a blameless and upright man' (Book of Job 1:1). He was wealthy and honoured. Then disaster struck. His great herds and flocks were destroyed; his many sons and daughters were killed when a violent wind demolished the house in which they were dining; finally Job's own flesh was invaded by loathsome sores.

Three of Job's friends came to comfort him. They tried to persuade Job that these evils had befallen him because of some sin he had committed. But Job insisted that his life had been blameless. He had cared for the poor and the fatherless; he had not spoken falsely; his heart had not been enticed by other women; he had never rejoiced at the ruin of an enemy; he had not departed from God's commandments.

Now Job is wretched. The people who once honoured him, regard him with contempt. He is repulsive even to his wife. God has 'broken him asunder' (ibid., 16:12).

Yet Job continues to insist that he is 'a just and blameless man'. He would like to speak with God – to *argue* his case before Him.

2

'I will say to God, do not condemn me; let me know why thou dost contend against me.' 'He will slay me; I have no hope; yet I will defend my ways to His face' (ibid., 10:2).

Then God answered Job. He reminded Job of His mighty deeds. He said to Job: 'Will you condemn me that you may be justified?' (ibid., 40:8). 'Who can stand before me? Who has given to me, that I should repay him? Whatever is under the whole heaven is mine' (ibid., 41:10–11).

Job was shaken. He said to God: 'I know that thou canst do all things, and no purpose of thine can be thwarted. . . . Therefore I have uttered what I did not understand, things too wonderful for me, which I did not know. . . . I had heard of thee by the hearing of the ear, but now my eye sees thee; therefore I despise myself, and repent in dust and ashes' (ibid., 42:2–6).

The Lord then turned His wrath against Job's three friends: 'for you have not spoken of me what is right, as my servant Job has' (ibid., 42:8).

What is the meaning of this myth? Why was God angry with the three friends? I think this was because they claimed that Job *must* have sinned in some way; *otherwise* God would not have overwhelmed him with calamities. God is rebuking them for their assumption that He must have some *reason* for what He does.

Why does God rebuke Job? I mean: what is He rebuking Job for? Not for sins in his life before evil befell him: but for Job's wishing to 'argue his case' with God; for wanting to know *why* God has brought disaster on him; for wanting to justify himself before God.

The significance of this ancient biblical drama, as I understand it, is that it displays something of the sense of the *concept* of God – or rather, of *a* concept of God. It shows that the notion of there being a *reason* for His deeds has no application to God; nor the notion of there being a *justification* or an *explanation* for God's actions. God stands in no need of justifying or of explaining His ways to mankind.

I will argue that there is an analogy between this conception of God, and Wittgenstein's view of the human 'language-games' and 'forms of life'.

It would be wrong to think that Wittgenstein was in general hostile to explanations. He was trained as an engineer in Germany. As a research student of aeronautics in Manchester, he experimented with kites, and he even designed and built an aircraft engine with reaction jets at the propeller tips. After his long service in the

3

First World War he spent two years fully engaged as an architect for the construction of a mansion in Vienna. In that capacity he would have sought explanations, e.g. of why one building material was acceptable and another not. In the Second World War he was a member of medical teams in London and Newcastle: he even devised a technique for determining the seriousness of different wounds. Throughout his life he maintained a keen interest in machines and physical mechanisms – wanting to understand how they functioned and what caused their failure to function.

It is not even true that in his philosophical work Wittgenstein was not interested in explanations. He was continuously seeking explanations for *philosophical perplexity*. In many writings, for example, he explored the question, 'How can I follow a rule?' He investigated the *question* – not in order to *answer* it – but to see what it *meant*. What seems to be the difficulty? We follow rules every day: what is the source of the puzzlement as to *how* this is possible?

Wittgenstein was singularly resourceful at *diagnosing* philosophical perplexities. He tried to explain their origins in terms of misleading pictures, half-articulated thoughts and assumptions. He tried to draw this submerged thinking, in himself and others, into the full light of day. In the whole history of philosophy there has never been so intensive a search for explanations of philosophical confusions.

When Wittgenstein wrote that in philosophy, 'We must do away with all explanation', this cannot be attributed to an eccentric dislike of explanations. The remark is an expression of Wittgenstein's conception of the peculiar nature of philosophy. I will propose that there is an analogy between his philosophical thought and religious thought, in respect to the attitude towards explanation. I think there are other analogies which will emerge later on.

First of all, however, I want to take up Wittgenstein's remark, 'I am not a religious man.' Actually, his life was one of exceptional striving for moral and spiritual purity – so much so, that I feel some doubt as to whether that assessment of himself was true. Or perhaps it would be better to say, I am uncertain as to how it should be *understood*. In the first chapter I will try to gain a perspective on this matter, by reviewing the evidences of religious thought and feeling in Wittgenstein's life – so far as they are known to us.

In subsequent chapters I will provide illustrations of explanation that are common in philosophy – and I will try to describe Wittgenstein's attitude toward those explanations, as it presents itself in his treatment of specific philosophical problems. Finally, I will summarize the analogies, as they appear to me, between Wittgenstein's view of philosophy and some characteristic features of religious thinking.

1

A RELIGIOUS MAN?

As a child Ludwig Wittgenstein received formal instruction in Roman Catholicism. Later on, conversations with his sister Gretl destroyed his childish faith. He became indifferent to, perhaps even contemptuous of, religious belief. When he was about 21 years of age, however, something occurred that had a lasting impact on him. He saw a play in Vienna which was mediocre drama: but there was a scene in which a person whose life had been desperately miserable, and who thought himself about to die, suddenly felt himself to be spoken to in the words, 'Nothing can happen to you!' No matter what occurred in the world, no harm could come to *him!* Wittgenstein was greatly struck by this thought (as he told me approximately forty years later): for the first time he perceived the possibility of religious belief (*NM*, p. 58).

In a 'Lecture on ethics' that Wittgenstein gave in Cambridge in 1929 (he was 40 years old), he spoke of an experience of his which he described as 'feeling *absolutely* safe. I mean the state of mind in which one is inclined to say, "I am safe, nothing can injure me whatever happens" ' (*LE*, p. 8). The words, 'I am safe; nothing can injure me', could strike one as an echo of Psalm 23: 'Yea, though I walk through the valley of the shadow of death, I will fear no evil: for thou art with me; thy rod and thy staff, they will comfort me.' In the same 'Lecture on ethics', Wittgenstein spoke of another experience he sometimes had, which could be described by the words, 'I wonder at the existence of the world.' He thought that this experience lay behind the idea that God created the world; that it was the experience of 'seeing the world as a miracle'. He also thought that

7

'the experience of absolute safety' was connected with the idea of 'feeling safe in the hands of God' (*LE*, p. 10).

Let us move to the First World War. Upon the declaration of war, Wittgenstein immediately volunteered for service as a private in the Austrian army, even though he could have been exempted because of a rupture. In September 1914 he discovered Tolstoy's *The Gospel in Brief* in a bookstore. Thereafter, 'He read and reread it, and had it always with him, under fire and at all times', and was known by the other soldiers as 'the one with the Gospels' (*McG*, p. 220). Near the end of the war, when Wittgenstein was in a prison camp at Monte Cassino, he and a fellow prisoner read Dostoevsky together. According to Parak, it was this writer's 'deeply religious attitude' that commended him to Wittgenstein. Parak believed that Wittgenstein had gone through a religious conversion in the war, and that this played a part in his subsequently giving away all of his inherited wealth (*McG*, p. 273).

Probably Wittgenstein's motivation for giving away his fortune was complex. (He once said to me that he had given away his wealth so that he would not have friends for the sake of his money.) But I think it is likely that Parak was right. Since Wittgenstein knew the Gospels thoroughly, he could hardly have failed to be struck by these words of Jesus:

> Truly I say to you, it will be hard for a rich man to enter the kingdom of heaven. Again I tell you, it is easier for a camel to go through the eye of a needle than for a rich man to enter the kingdom of God.
>
> (*Matthew* 19:23–4)

> Whoever of you does not renounce all that he has cannot be my disciple.
>
> (*Luke* 14:13)

The diaries that Wittgenstein kept during the war reveal that he often prayed, not that he should be spared from death, but that he should meet it without cowardice and without losing control of himself.

> How will I behave when it comes to shooting? I am not afraid of being shot but of not doing my duty properly. God give me strength! Amen!
>
> If it is all over with me now, may I die a good death, mindful of myself. May I never lose myself! Now I might have

8

the opportunity to be a decent human being, because I am face to face with death. May the spirit enlighten me.

(*McG*, p. 221)

Brian McGuinness, biographer of Wittgenstein, says: 'Generally before action he prays like this: God be with me! The spirit be with me!' (ibid.). Wittgenstein volunteered for the extremely dangerous post of artillery observer in an advanced position. He wrote: 'Perhaps nearness to death will bring light into my life' (ibid., p. 240).

While he was in prison camp Wittgenstein had to think ahead to what his vocation would be when he was released. Probably he had already decided to renounce his fortune – which he insisted on, once he was back in Vienna, despite the amazed protests of his family. He could not return to philosophy because he felt that he had nothing more to say. The choice was between the priesthood and the life of a schoolmaster. The four years of theological studies required for the priesthood ruled out that option for him. He decided to become a school teacher. To his friend Parak he said: 'I'd most like to be a priest, but when I'm a teacher I can read the Gospel with the children' (ibid., p. 274).

During the war Wittgenstein and Paul Engelmann, the architect, had become friends. In his *Memoir* of Wittgenstein, Engelmann raises the question, 'Was Wittgenstein religious?' His answer is that the idea of God as creator of the world scarcely engaged Wittgenstein's attention, but 'the notion of a last judgment was of profound concern to him' (*Engel*, p. 77). When I knew Wittgenstein, many years later, I had the same impression. To quote from my *Memoir*:

> Wittgenstein did once say that he thought he could understand the conception of God, in so far as it is involved in one's awareness of one's own sin and guilt. He added that he could not understand the conception of a *Creator*. I think the ideas of Divine judgment, forgiveness, and redemption had some intelligibility for him, as being related in his mind to feelings of disgust with himself, an intense desire for purity, and a sense of the helplessness of human beings to make themselves better.
>
> Wittgenstein once suggested that a way in which the notion of immortality can acquire a meaning is through one's feeling that one has duties from which one cannot be released, even by death. Wittgenstein himself possessed a stern sense of duty.

I believe that Wittgenstein was prepared by his own character and experience to comprehend the idea of a judging and
redeeming God. But any cosmological conception of a Deity,
derived from the notions of cause or of infinity, would be
repugnant to him.

(NM, p. 59)

The influence of the notion of a Last Judgment is reflected in some of
his remarks. The first occurs in a letter to me in 1940: 'May I not
prove too much of a skunk when I shall be tried' (ibid., Letter 3, p.
88). The second was in a conversation between Drury and Wittgenstein in 1949. Drury had mentioned a doctrine of Origen, according to
which 'at the end of time there would be a final restitution of all
things. That even Satan and the fallen angels would be restored to
their former glory.' Drury then added that this conception 'was at
once condemned as heretical'. Wittgenstein replied: 'Of course it was
rejected. It would make nonsense of everything else. If what we do
now is to make no difference in the end, then all the seriousness of life
is done away with' (R, pp. 174–5). The third remark was written in
1951 in the final months of his life: 'God can say to me: "I am judging
you out of your own mouth. Your own actions have made you shud-
der with disgust when you have seen them in others" ' (VB, p. 87).
The Tractatus Notebooks and the Tractatus itself were written while
Wittgenstein was serving in the Great War. Both works contain
thoughts of a religious nature. In the Notebooks of 1916 he puts the
question, 'What do I know about God and the purpose of life?' (NB,
p. 73). He goes on to say that 'something about the world is problematic, which we call its meaning'; that 'to pray is to think about the
meaning of life'; and that 'to believe in God means to see that life has
a meaning' (NB, p. 74). In the Tractatus he says: 'God does not reveal
himself in the world' (T, 6.432). 'The mystical is not how the world is,
but that it is' (T, 6.44). The second of these statements is connected
with 'the experience of wondering at the existence of the world', and
the experience of 'seeing the world as a miracle', to which he referred
in the 'Lecture on ethics' of 1929.

M. O' C. Drury and Wittgenstein first met in 1929. Their friendship continued throughout Wittgenstein's life. Drury was in his first
year as an undergraduate at Cambridge, and had begun to attend the
lectures of G. E. Moore. In his first lecture Moore said that among
the subjects on which he was required to lecture was the philosophy
of religion, but that he would not be talking about this because he

had nothing to say. Drury was indignant that a Professor of Philosophy should be silent on so important a subject, and said so to Wittgenstein. Wittgenstein's reply was to quote from Augustine's *Confessions*, 'And woe to those who say nothing concerning thee, just because the chatterboxes talk a lot of nonsense.' He added, 'I won't refuse to talk to you about God or about religion' (*R*, p. 104).

Drury once remarked how impressed he was by the ancient liturgical prayers of the Latin rite and their translation in the Anglican prayer book. Wittgenstein replied: 'Yes, those prayers read as if they had been soaked in centuries of worship. When I was a prisoner of war in Italy we were compelled to attend Mass on Sundays. I was very glad of that compulsion' (*R*, p. 109). Wittgenstein and Drury had a talk about Drury's intention to be ordained as a priest. Wittgenstein said:

> Just think, Drury, what it would mean to have to preach a sermon every week; you couldn't do it. I would be afraid that you would try and give some sort of philosophical justification for Christian beliefs, as if some sort of proof was needed.... The symbolisms of Catholicism are wonderful beyond words. But any attempt to make it into a philosophical system is offensive. All religions are wonderful, even those of the most primitive tribes. The ways in which people express their religious feelings differ enormously.
>
> (*R*, p. 123)

In another conversation Wittgenstein made these remarks:

> But remember that Christianity is not a matter of saying a lot of prayers; in fact we are told not to do that. If you and I are to live religious lives, it mustn't be that we talk a lot about religion, but that our manner of life is different. It is my belief that only if you try to be helpful to other people will you in the end find your way to God.
>
> (*R*, p. 129)

As Drury was leaving Wittgenstein suddenly said: 'There is a sense in which you and I are both Christians' (*R*, p. 130).

I do not know what Wittgenstein specifically had in mind when he said that 'we are told' not to say a 'lot of prayers'. There are, however, many biblical admonishments of those who cry out in words of prayer and praise, but do not alter the manner of their lives. Jeremiah said:

11

> Thus says the Lord of hosts, the God of Israel, Amend your ways and your doings, and I will let you dwell in this place. Do not trust in these deceptive words: 'This is the temple of the Lord, the temple of the Lord, the temple of the Lord.'
>
> For if you truly amend your ways and your doings, if you truly execute justice one with another, if you do not oppress the alien, the fatherless or the widow, or shed innocent blood in this place, and if you do not go after other gods to your own hurt, then I will let you dwell in this place, in the land that I gave of old to your fathers for ever.
>
> *(Jeremiah* 7:3–7).

And there are these words of Jesus:

> Not every one who says to me, 'Lord, Lord', shall enter the kingdom of heaven, but he who does the will of my Father who is in heaven. On that day many will say to me, 'Lord, Lord, did we not prophesy in your name, and cast out demons in your name, and do many mighty works in your name?' And then I will declare to them, 'I never knew you; depart from me, you evildoers'.
>
> *(Matthew* 7:21–3)

> Why do you call me 'Lord, Lord', and not do what I tell you?
>
> *(Luke* 6:46)

What is being said is not, of course, that worship and praise have no place in a religious life, but rather that they are worthless if there is no amending one's ways and one's doings.

In 1931 Wittgenstein lived for a while in his hut in Norway. On his return to Cambridge he told Drury that he had done no philosophical writing, but had spent the time in prayer. He had written a confession of those things in his past life of which he was most ashamed. He insisted that Drury read it. He asked Moore to do the same. Several years later he made what was possibly the same confession, to Fania Pascal, but that time orally, face to face. We will come to that episode later.

By 1933 Drury had decided against training for the priesthood. Instead, with Wittgenstein's encouragement and financial help, he undertook medical training. One day in 1936 he told Wittgenstein that he had been asked to be a godfather at the christening of his nephew. Drury went on to say:

The godparents have to promise in the child's name 'To renounce the devil and all his works, the pomps and vanities of this wicked world, and all the sinful lusts of the flesh'. I feel it would be hypocrisy for me to speak those words. It is something that I haven't done myself.

Wittgenstein replied: 'To renounce the pomps and vanities of this wicked world. Just think what that would really involve. Who of us today even thinks of such a thing? We all want to be admired (*R*, p. 153). In 1944 Drury was serving in a military hospital in Wales. When Wittgenstein came to Wales they were able to spend some time together. Wittgenstein told Drury that one of his students had written to him to tell him that he had become a Roman Catholic. Wittgenstein went on to say: 'I seem to be surrounded now by Roman Catholic converts. I don't know whether they pray for me. I hope they do' (*R*, p. 163). In the invasion of France, Drury was to be a medical officer on a landing craft. When they said goodbye, Wittgenstein remarked: 'If it ever happens that you get mixed up in hand to hand fighting, you must just stand aside and let yourself be massacred' (*R*, p. 163). In 1949 Wittgenstein said to Drury: 'I thought when I gave up my professorship that I had at last got rid of my vanity. Now I find I am vain about the style in which I am able to write' (*R*, p. 175). When the two were comparing the Gospels, Wittgenstein said that his favourite was the Gospel according to St Matthew. He added that he found it difficult to understand the Fourth Gospel, as contrasted with the Synoptic Gospels. But he went on to say: 'If you can accept the miracle that God became man, then all of these difficulties are as nothing. For then it is impossible for me to say what form the record of such an event should take (*R*, p. 178). Wittgenstein once remarked to Drury that Drury had had 'a most remarkable life': first, his years of studying philosophy in Cambridge; then his training in medicine; then the war; and now his new work in psychiatry. Drury replied that one thing he felt was wrong was that he had not lived a religious life. Wittgenstein said: 'It has troubled me that, in some way I never intended, your getting to know me has made you less religious than you would have been had you never met me' (*R*, p. 179). In the same year Wittgenstein said to Drury:

I have had a letter from an old friend in Austria, a priest. In it he says he hopes my work will go well, if it should be God's will. Now that is all I want: if it should be God's will. Bach wrote on the title page of his *Orgelbüchlein*, 'To the glory of the

13

most high God, and that my neighbour may be benefited thereby'. That is what I would have liked to say about my work.

(R, pp. 181–2)

In 1951 Wittgenstein knew that his death was close at hand. He continued to work hard. He said to Drury: 'Isn't it curious that although I know I have not long to live, I never find myself thinking about a "future life". All my interest is still on this life and the writing I am still able to do' (R, p. 183). Let us turn to the 'confession' that Wittgenstein wrote out in Norway in 1931 and that he requested be read by several of his friends. What was the motive for this extraordinary action? Rush Rhees takes up this question and shows it to have an unexpected moral depth (R, 'Postscript', pp. 190–219). Wittgenstein wrote in his letters and private notes that he wanted to become a different man, to be utterly honest with himself, to yield no longer to self-deception. He believed that such a change could be produced, not by a merely intellectual examination of himself, but only by an act of courage – by forcing himself to do something that was terribly difficult for him. In the First World War he volunteered for the most dangerous post in the hope that coming face to face with death would make him a better person. In much the same way, years later, he resolved to make a confession to people who knew him: this painful action might help to rid him of his 'falsity'.

In 1931, the year he wrote a confession in Norway, he also wrote in a notebook: 'A confession must be part of the new life' (VB, p. 18). In a notebook of 1937 he wrote:

> Last year with God's help I pulled myself together and made a confession. This brought me into more settled waters, into a better relation with people, and to greater seriousness, but now it is as though I had spent all that, and I am not far from where I was before.

(R, pp. 191–2)

In the 1930s Wittgenstein had decided to visit Russia. A necessary part of his preparation was to learn Russian. Fania Pascal gave him private teaching in Cambridge. One day in 1937 he phoned her to say that he had to see her urgently. On arriving he said, 'I have come to make a confession.' According to Mrs Pascal, he spoke with composure during the first part of the confession, the substance of

14

which was that he believed that most people who knew him, took him to be in racial inheritance more Aryan than Jewish; whereas the opposite was true, and he had done nothing to prevent this misapprehension (*R*, p. 48).

At one stage Mrs Pascal cried out: 'What is it? You want to be perfect?' Wittgenstein replied: '*Of course* I want to be perfect!' (*R*, p. 50).

The rest of the confession was more difficult. In Mrs Pascal's words:

> The most painful part of the confession came at the end, a traumatic experience to re-live and own up to. I recall well that at this stage he had to keep a firmer control on himself, telling in a clipped way of the cowardly shameful manner in which he had behaved. During the short period when he was teaching in a village school in Austria, he hit a little girl and hurt her (my memory is, without details, of a physically violent act). When she ran to the headmaster to complain, Wittgenstein denied he had done it. The event stood out as a crisis of his early manhood. It may have been this that made him give up teaching, perhaps made him realise that he ought to live as a solitary.
>
> (*R*, pp. 50–1)

The incident of lying apparently entered into the confessions of 1931 as well as of 1937. It was a burden that pressed on Wittgenstein and at times became unbearable. Surely he felt the drastic act of confession to be *demanded* of him, and to be the only way to a 'new life'.

So far I have been providing a summary of incidents in Wittgenstein's life, and of thoughts of his that were expressed in conversation, in wartime personal notebooks, in the *Tractatus* and the *Tractatus Notebooks*, and in the 'Lecture on ethics' – incidents and thoughts that had religious meaning.

I turn now to another source. In his notebooks and manuscripts, after his return to philosophical research in 1929, Wittgenstein wrote many remarks that did not belong directly to his philosophical work. They deal with many topics: music, architecture, poetry, genius, tragedy, race, culture. Some of them are *about* religion – but some are in themselves religious thoughts. The selection of these remarks was given by G. H. von Wright from a great mass of material, and was published under the title *Vermischte Bemerkungen*

(*Miscellaneous Remarks*) in 1977. It was published in a second edition in 1980 with English translation by Peter Winch, under the title *Culture and Value*.

The reflections on religious topics which I am bringing together here, have an especially high value because, first, they were written during the period in which Wittgenstein was creating his new philosophical outlook – and, second, since these remarks were interspersed with his concentrated writings on philosophical problems, one can expect them to be a product of the same energy and depth of thought. The remarks I shall quote date from 1929 to shortly before Wittgenstein's death in 1951.

In 1929 Wittgenstein wrote: 'If something is good it is also divine. In a strange way this sums up my ethics. Only the supernatural can express the Supernatural' (*VB*, p. 3). We jump now to 1937 for an observation about Christianity:

> Christianity is not a doctrine; I mean, not a theory about what has happened and will happen with the human soul, but a description of an actual occurrence in human life. For 'consciousness of sin' is an actual occurrence, and so are despair and salvation through faith. Those who speak of these things (like Bunyan) are simply describing what has happened to them, whatever anyone may want to say about it.
>
> (*VB*, p. 28)

Here is a comparison of the Gospels with Paul's letters:

> The spring which flows quietly and transparently through the Gospels seems to have *foam* on it in Paul's Epistles. Or, that is how it seems to *me*. Perhaps it is just my own impurity which sees cloudiness in it; for why shouldn't this impurity be able to pollute what is clear? But *to me* it's as if I saw human passion here, something like pride or anger, which does not agree with the humility of the *Gospels*. As if there were here an emphasis on his own person, *and even as a religious act*, which is foreign to the Gospel. . . .
>
> In the Gospels – so it seems to me – everything is *less* pretentious, humbler, simpler. *There* are huts; with Paul a church. There all men are equal and God himself is a man; with Paul there is already something like a hierarchy; honours and offices. – That is, as it were, what my *nose* tells me.
>
> (*VB*, p. 30)

Another reflection on Christianity:

> Christianity is not based on a historical truth; rather, it gives us a (historical) narrative and says: now believe! But not, believe this narrative with the belief appropriate to a historical narrative – rather: believe, through thick and thin, and you can do that only as the result of a life. *Here you have a narrative – don't take the same attitude to it as to another historical narrative!* Give it an *entirely different* place in your life. – There is nothing *paradoxical* in that!
>
> (*VB*, p. 32)

We are given a passionate account of why he is inclined to believe in the Resurrection:

> What inclines even me to believe in Christ's Resurrection? It is as though I play with the thought. – If he did not rise from the dead, then he decomposed in the grave like any other man. *He is dead and decomposed.* In that case he is a teacher like any other and can no longer *help*; and once more we are orphaned and alone. And must content ourselves with wisdom and speculation. We are as it were in a hell, where we can only dream, and are as it were cut off from heaven by a roof. But if I am to be *really* saved – then I need *certainty* – not wisdom, dreams, speculation – and this certainty is faith. And faith is faith in what my heart, my *soul* needs, not my speculative intelligence. For it is my soul, with its passions, as it were with its flesh and blood, that must be saved, not my abstract mind.
>
> (*VB*, p. 33)

In 1944 he wrote: 'People are religious to the extent that they believe themselves to be not so much *imperfect*, as *ill*. . . . Any half-way decent man will think himself extremely imperfect, but a religious man believes himself *wretched*' (*VB*, p. 45). And again:

> The Christian religion is only for one who needs infinite help, therefore only for one who feels an infinite need. The whole planet cannot be in greater anguish than a *single* soul. The Christian faith – as I view it – is the refuge in this ultimate anguish.
>
> To whom it is given in this anguish to open his heart, instead of contracting it, accepts the means of salvation in his heart.
>
> (*VB*, p. 46)

17

In 1946 he writes:

> One of the things Christianity says, I think, is that all sound doctrines are of no avail. One must change one's *life*. (Or the *direction* of one's life.)
>
> That all wisdom is cold; and that one can no more use it to bring one's life into order than one can forge *cold* iron.
>
> A sound doctrine does not have to *catch hold* of one; one can follow it like a doctor's prescription. – But here something must grasp one and turn one around. – (This is how I understand it.) Once turned around, one must *stay* turned around.
>
> Wisdom is passionless. In contrast faith is what Kierkegaard calls a *passion*.
>
> (*VB*, p. 53)

In 1947 he wrote the following about his philosophical work:

> Is what I am doing really worth the labour? Surely only if it receives a light from above. And if that happens – why should I worry about the fruits of my work being stolen? If what I am writing is really of value, how could anyone steal the value from me? If the light from above is *not* there, then I cannot be any more than clever.
>
> (*VB*, pp. 57-8)

This reference to his worry that the fruits of his work might be stolen, reflects the same anxiety that he expressed in the Preface to the *Investigations*. He said there that he had learned that 'my results (which I had communicated in lectures, typescripts and discussions), variously misunderstood, more or less mangled or watered down, were in circulation. This stung my vanity and I had difficulty in quieting it' (*PI*, Preface, p. ix).

What is especially interesting, however, for my present purpose, is his remark that his philosophical labour, which was truly enormous, is of value 'only if it receives a light from above'. What is the meaning of this phrase 'a light from above'? I am sure that it had a religious meaning. It reminds me of the words of James in his Epistle: 'Every good endowment and every perfect gift is from above, coming down from the Father of lights with whom there is no variation or shadow due to change' (*James* 1:17). In 1948 Wittgenstein wrote: 'Religious faith and superstition are entirely different. One of them springs from *fear* and is a kind of false science.

18

The other is a trusting' (*VB*, p. 72). In 1950 he wrote the following about 'proofs' of God's existence:

> A proof of God's existence should really be something by which one could convince oneself of God's existence. But I think that *believers* who have provided such proofs, have wanted to give their 'belief' an intellectual analysis and foundation, although they themselves would never have come to believe through such proofs. Perhaps one could 'convince someone of God's existence' through a certain kind of upbringing, by shaping his life in such and such a way.
>
> Life can educate one to a belief in God. And also *experiences* can do this; but not visions and other forms of sense experience which show us the 'existence of this being' – but, e.g. sufferings of various kinds. These neither show us God in the way a sense impression shows us an object, nor do they give rise to *conjectures* about him. Experiences, thoughts, – life can force this concept on us.
>
> (*VB*, pp. 85–6)

It was Wittgenstein's constant view that none of the famous philosophical proofs of the existence of God could bring anyone to believe in God. When Drury still had the intention to become a priest, Wittgenstein warned him against trying to give a philosophical justification for Christian belief, 'as if some sort of proof was needed'. Once I quoted to him a remark of Kierkegaard which went something like this: 'How can it be that Christ does not exist, since I know that He has saved me?' Wittgenstein's response was: 'You see! It isn't a question of *proving* anything!' He thought that the symbolisms of religion are 'wonderful'; but he distrusted theological formulations. He objected to the idea that Christianity is a 'doctrine', i.e. a theory about what has happened and will happen to the human soul. Instead it is a description of actual occurrences in the lives of some people – of 'consciousness of sin', of despair, of salvation through faith. For Wittgenstein the emphasis in religious belief had to be on doing – on 'amending one's ways', 'turning one's life around'. No *doctrine*, no matter how sound, had the power to bring that about.

The insistence that how one lives and acts must be *radically* different if one is to be saved, is indeed the authentic teaching of Jesus:

Love your enemies, do good to those who hate you, bless those who curse you, pray for those who abuse you. To him who strikes you on the cheek, offer the other also; and from him who takes away your cloak do not withhold your coat as well. Give to every one who begs from you; and of him who takes away your goods, do not ask them again. And as you wish that men would do to you, do so to them.

(Luke 6:27–31)

Truly, truly, I say to you, he who believes in me will also do the works that I do.

(John 14:12)

If you love me, you will keep my commandments.

(John 14:15)

If you keep my commandments, you will abide in my love.

(John 15:10)

And James in his Epistle says:

What does it profit, my brethren, if a man says he has faith but has not works? Can his faith save him? If a brother or sister is ill-clad and in lack of daily food, and one of you says to them, 'Go in peace, be warmed and filled', without giving them the things needed for the body, what does it profit? So faith by itself if it has no works, is dead.

(James 2:14–17)

For Wittgenstein the essential thing in a religious life was not the acceptance of doctrines or creeds, but *works*. To Drury he said that his belief was that 'only if you try to be helpful to other people will you in the end find your way to God'.

Wittgenstein even seemed to think that religious life did not depend on churches. He said to Drury:

For all you and I can tell, the religion of the future will be without any priests or ministers. I think one of the things you and I have to learn is that we have to live without the consolation of belonging to a church.

(R, p. 129)

Did he think that people in general might reach the stage of living religiously without the institution of churches; or only that this was

20

possible for some? His religious sense was Christian; but he distrusted institutions.

On the other hand, he admired the celebrations, rituals, symbols, which characterize religious practices in churches. What he thought to be a mistake is the idea that these are *founded* on propositions which the worshippers believe to be true. In his remarks on Frazer's *Golden Bough* he says: 'A religious symbol does not rest on any *opinion*!' (*RFG*, p. 3). If there is no opinion, then there is no *false* opinion. Wittgenstein likens a religious symbol to a *gesture*. 'What we have in the ancient rites is the practice of a highly cultivated gesture-language' (ibid., p. 10). Placing flowers on a grave is not based on the belief that the soul of the departed will perceive the flowers and delight in them. This action is a gesture of respect – a way of honouring the dead. It is not based on any belief – any more than is a greeting.

Let me summarize what we know of the emotions, thoughts and deeds of Wittgenstein's life which had a religious meaning. The feeling of being 'absolutely safe', which first came to him at about age 21, exerted some hold on him throughout most of his life. The desire to become 'a decent human being' was vividly expressed in his prayers during the First World War, and in his volunteering for a dangerous post. The act of renouncing his inherited wealth probably had, in part, a religious motive. At the end of the war his first preference for a vocation was to be a priest. His discussions with Drury contained many reflections on religious matters. His 'confessions' belonged to a hope for 'a new life'. He expected and feared a Last Judgment. He read and reread the Gospels and knew them thoroughly. His desire for his philosophical work was that it should be 'God's will'. He thought it would be of value only if it received 'a light from above'. His conception of the meaning of Christianity stressed human 'wretchedness' and 'anguish' – and the necessity of 'turning around' and 'opening one's heart'. This surely expressed an awareness of his own state and his own need.

Considering all of this, it is surely right to say that Wittgenstein's mature life was strongly marked by religious thought and feeling. I am inclined to think that he was more deeply religious than are many people who correctly regard themselves as religious believers.

If this is so, how are we to take Wittgenstein's statement: 'I am not a religious man'? Perhaps part of his meaning might be that he did not belong to a church nor engage in any formal religious devotions: Indeed, I think, this would have been impossible for him. But at most this would be only a part of what he meant.

More important would be the fact that Wittgenstein had rigorous critical standards. This was so in music, art, literature, architecture, poetry, philosophy. Certainly he did not regard his own philosophical work as 'great', or even as 'good'. In regard to his conception of 'a religious life' he would employ the same severe standards. His models of truly religious men were St Augustine, John Bunyan, St Francis, George Fox. In comparison with those great religious figures he would regard his own religious life as mediocre. He judged himself to be vain, desirous of admiration, easily given to irritation, anger, contempt for others. He knew that he had not 'turned around', had not 'opened his heart'.

Also Wittgenstein may have believed that he did not give enough space in his life to prayer and religious reflection. His thinking was concentrated on philosophical problems. He worked with furious intensity. He produced a vast amount of writing, which was a flood of singular turns of thought and stunning analogies. He lived under a tension of discipline, with only moments of relaxation.

We may see here a way of understanding his remark of 1946: 'I cannot kneel to pray because it's as though my knees are stiff. I am afraid of disintegration (of my disintegration), if I became soft' (*VB*, p. 56). From a lecture by Professor Roy Holland, I obtained a suggestion (which I hope I have rightly understood) as to a possible meaning of this remark. Wittgenstein lived as if the philosophical work that wholly absorbed him, was *demanded* of him. His whole life was dedicated to it. He had the sense of a duty *imposed* on him. To do this work he held himself in constant tension, always *engaged*, never allowing the problems to slip from his grasp, forever trying out new analogies, fresh comparisons. This search for insight was unremitting.

Probably Wittgenstein realized that if he gave himself to prayer with the intensity this would require, an intensity that was characteristic of every work he undertook – then he would 'disintegrate'. That is, his philosophical concentration would be disturbed. The 'stiff knees' may be a metaphor for his stern posture of total engagement. Becoming 'soft' would mean losing the tautness, the fighting alertness, that was required for him to pursue his ceaseless battles with the traps of language.

I take this remark of Wittgenstein's to imply that he had an *impulse* to kneel in prayer, an impulse that he resisted in order to maintain that mental concentration, that drawing together of his powers into a single burning point, which was demanded by his philosophical commitment.

Wittgenstein had an intense desire for moral and spiritual purity. '*Of course* I want to be perfect!' he exclaimed. This was not arrogance – for he knew he was far from perfect. He struggled to subdue the anxiety that his thoughts would be appropriated by others and passed off as their own. This was part of what he called his 'vanity'. He fought against this worldly anxiety, but not with complete success.

He judged himself to be neither a creative philosopher, nor a religious person. On the first matter he was surely wrong. The second matter is not within our competence to determine. But we can say with confidence that he knew the demands of religion. And certainly he was as qualified as any philosopher ever has been, to understand what it might mean to see the problems of philosophy from a religious point of view.

2

THE SEARCH FOR EXPLANATION

Wittgenstein did much religious thinking: but religious thoughts do not figure in his detailed treatments of the philosophical problems. It would seem, therefore, that when he spoke of seeing those problems 'from a religious point of view', he did not mean that he conceived of them as religious problems, but instead that there was a similarity, or similarities, between his conception of philosophy and something that is characteristic of religious thinking. In the introduction I suggested that Wittgenstein's views of *explanation* may provide one point of similarity.

The word 'explanation' ranges over a vast number of different activities. There are explanations of how to do things – to brush one's teeth, to sail a kite, to swim on one's back. There are explanations of how a mechanism works. There are explanations of why one should not act in a certain way; of why one should apologize; of why one should not dress like that, should be on time, should be polite. And so on. It seems that there is nothing whatever that does not get explained in one way or another.

The empirical sciences seek explanations. This may take the form of a search for *laws* – in mechanics, laws of motion; in psychology, laws of association, or of operant conditioning. Sometimes science seeks not laws, but instead the composition of things – in chemistry, the composition of salt or of water; in physics, the composition of the atom; in psychology, the components and processes that 'constitute' perception or memory.

Philosophy is not an empirical science. But from antiquity it has been dominated by a tradition of explanation. Philosophers have been fascinated and perplexed by concepts, such as *beauty, justice, knowledge*. They have wanted to find out what justice or beauty or knowledge *is*. Their concentration, however, was not on doings or happenings in the world, but on the *meaning* of these words. When you say that you 'know' this or that, what are you *saying?* Usually the concentration was on *truth-conditions*. When you say that you *know* that so-and-so, what are the necessary and sufficient conditions that must be satisfied in order for your assertion to be true? If a philosopher could spell out those conditions he would be giving a *definition* of the meaning of 'know'. He would have given a logical analysis, or a philosophical analysis, of *knowledge*. This would be an 'explanation' of what knowledge is, what it consists of. It is a different form of explanation than occurs in chemistry or physics, and a different kind of analysis: but still it would be analysis and explanation.

LAWS OF NATURE

In expounding Wittgenstein's thinking about 'explanation' let us begin with his attitude toward the explanation of natural phenomena by laws of nature. This attitude is expressed in his *Tractatus* and was renewed in his later philosophical thinking. In the *Tractatus* he says:

> The whole modern conception of the world is founded on the illusion that the so-called laws of nature are the explanation of natural phenomena.
>
> (*T*, 6.371)

> Thus people today stop at the laws of nature, treating them as something inviolable, just as God and Fate were treated in past ages.
>
> And indeed both are right and both wrong. The view of the ancients is, however, decidedly clearer in that they acknowledge a clear terminus, while the modern system would make it look as if it explained *everything*.
>
> (*T*, 6.372)

It does not seem to me that these two numbers are saying exactly the same thing. In 6.371 it is said that it is an illusion to suppose that the phenomena of nature are explained by the laws of nature. The implication is that the laws of nature do not explain anything. The meaning of 6.372 seems not to be that the laws of nature do not, in

25

any way, explain natural phenomena. Instead the point is that explanations have to come to an end, and that in which they end is not itself explained: not *everything* is explained.

Many years later, in one of his classes of the academic year 1946–47, Wittgenstein said similar things about the relation of natural law to explanation. I will summarize some of Wittgenstein's remarks, as they were recorded by Yorick Smythies. [1]

Wittgenstein said that it was an absurd mistake to suppose that natural laws *compel* things to happen the way they happen. If the law of gravitation holds, that just means that a body moves according to the law of gravitation. 'What on earth would it mean that the natural law compels a thing to go as it goes?' A natural law is only a description of a regularity in nature. The idea that natural laws compel events comes in part from the use of the world 'law'; for this word suggests more than an observed regularity which we expect to continue. The words 'natural law' also seem to be linked in people's minds with 'a certain kind of fatalism. What will happen is laid down somewhere.' 'The notion of compulsion is there if you think of the regularity as compelled; as produced by rails. If, besides the notion of regularity, you bring in the notion of "It must move like this because the rails are laid like this".'

Wittgenstein's thinking here is clear and correct. What is called a 'law of nature' is nothing but a description of an observed pattern in nature. A law of nature cannot show that a certain occurrence *had* to happen. Nor can anything show that a natural law *has* to exist. One natural law may be 'explained' by being subsumed under another natural law. This is bringing a certain regularity in nature under another, more comprehensive, regularity. But there can be no demonstration that either regularity had to exist. One may be tempted to say that natural science only describes and does not explain; but this can be misleading, for it suggests that there *could be* an 'explanation' of a kind that consists in showing that a particular natural phenomenon had to occur, or in showing that a particular regularity in nature had to exist.

There is a perfect agreement between the *Tractatus* and Wittgenstein's subsequent thinking about laws of nature. But the *Tractatus* says something else, concerning explanation, which the *Investigations* rejects. The *Tractatus* says: 'It is clear that there are no grounds for believing that the simplest eventuality will actually be realized' (*T*, 6.3631). Here Wittgenstein was saying that there never are any *grounds* for believing that such-and-such will occur. Suppose a farmer believes that it will rain in June because it has rained in every June for the past twenty years. His belief may be wrong; but surely he has *grounds* for that belief. In the *Investigations* Wittgenstein says:

> If anyone said that information about the past could not convince him that something would happen in the future, I should not understand him. One might ask him: What do you expect to be told then? What sort of information do you call a ground for such a belief? What do you call 'conviction'? In what kind of way do you expect to be convinced? – If *these* are not grounds, then what are grounds? – If you say these are not grounds, then you must surely be able to state what must be the case for us to have the right to say that there are grounds for our assumption.
>
> For note: Grounds here are not propositions which logically imply what is believed.

(PI, 481)

Wittgenstein is here combating a position that he took in his first book. In the *Tractatus* he was implying that no information about the past could be 'grounds' for the belief that it will rain next June. Apparently he had lost sight of the actual use of the word 'grounds'. As Wittgenstein says in the *Investigations*: 'This sort of statement about the past is simply what we call a ground for assuming that this will happen in the future' *(PI, 480)*.

PHILOSOPHICAL ANALYSIS

In its attempt to understand perplexing concepts, philosophy has sought to 'analyse' those concepts. A concept is not a particular occurrence in the world, nor a state of something. It is the meaning of a word. The concept of justice is the meaning of the word 'justice'; the concept of anger is the meaning of the word 'anger'; the concept of truth is the meaning of the word 'truth'. It is characteristic of philosophy that one is confused by the meaning of a word. Since ancient times it has been assumed that the only way to remove this confusion is to produce a correct *definition* of the confusing word. A definition of the word would be, at the same time, a definition of the concept expressed by the word. It could be called an 'analytic definition', since it would be achieved by an analysis of the truth-conditions for the application of the word. A proposed definition is commonly called a 'theory'. A proposal about how to define *justice* would be 'a theory of justice'. The programme for philosophy was to formulate theories of *perception*, of *memory*, of *intention*, and so on. A philosophical theory of *memory* would not rely on research in laboratories on human or animal subjects. A philosophy of memory would not be .concerned with the empirical conditions that might promote or interfere with accurate remembering. The philosophical theory would be concerned solely with the *meaning* of the words 'memory', 'remember', and their cognates. What, for example, are the conditions that must be satisfied if the statement, 'He remembered such-and-such', is true?

The conception that philosophy was engaged in analysing the meaning of linguistic expressions had the obvious implication that philosophers must, or should, pay close attention to how those expressions are *actually used* by the speakers of the language. Philosophy had to focus on language. For a period in this century the phrase 'linguistic philosophy' was used to designate the kind of philosophical work that was centred on language. This locution seems to have dropped out of use, perhaps because it was gradually realized that there was no alternative to 'linguistic' philosophy.

As philosophy became more and more oriented towards language, problems about the nature of language itself came to the fore. A sentence is, in a sense, only a string of marks on paper, or a sequence of sounds. How can a person, by uttering a sentence, *say* something – give some information, make an assertion or a statement? What *is* 'saying'? What distinguishes a meaningful utterance from a meaningless one?

Suppose that you made a gesture towards two people, A and B, and said 'Come here'. A comes forward. You say, 'No. I meant B.' What took place, which consisted in your meaning B and not A? (see *Z*, 22). Was it something that went on in your mind, when you made that gesture and uttered the words, 'Come here'?

Is the meaning, or 'sense', of a sentence determined by something other than truth-conditions? Do truth-conditions come into it at all? What is 'the general concept' of the meaning or sense of sentences? How does a sentence express a *thought*? What is the composition of a thought? How are thoughts, and the sentences that express them, related to reality? In what does the truth or falsity of thought and statements consist?

Questions such as these were the problems with which philosophy began to wrestle. One could say that the fundamental problem which confronted philosophical analysis was, 'What is the essential nature of language, and of expression in language?'

THE PICTURE-THEORY OF THE *TRACTATUS*

Wittgenstein's first book, written largely while he was in the Austrian army during the First World War, belongs to the tradition of philosophical analysis. It presents an original and comprehensive theory of the nature of language, of the nature of thought and of the nature of reality. The treatment in the *Tractatus* of these abstract and highly general concepts, was the high tide of philosophical analysis. In January 1915 Wittgenstein wrote in his *Tractatus Notebooks*: 'My *whole* task consists in explaining the nature of propositions. That means, to give the nature of all facts, whose picture a proposition *is*. To give the nature of all being' (*NB*, p. 39). One of the most dazzling conceptions of the *Tractatus* is that a 'proposition' is a *picture*. There can be problems as to what a 'proposition' is. The German word *Satz*, translated here as 'proposition', is the ordinary German for 'sentence'. So one can think of a 'proposition' as, first of all, a sentence. But one can construct meaningless sentences, and they would not be propositions. Nor would questions or exclamations be propositions. A proposition would be a meaningful sentence that is used to assert or affirm something, or to describe some state of affairs. 'She wore a hat', 'He complained of a headache' – these would be propositions. The conception of the *Tractatus* is that both of these propositions, or statements, are *pictures*. Pictures of what? Pictures of situations in the world – pictures of states of affairs. They may be correct or incorrect pictures – true or false – but they are pictures. One of the main undertakings of the *Tractatus* was to explain how a sentence of language could depict, or picture, a state of affairs in the world. The account of this in the *Tractatus* is fascinating. I will expound this conception as concisely as I can.

According to the *Tractatus* the objects, or things, that exist in the world, are either simple or complex. The notion of a 'simple object' is a striking conception. A simple object has ·no kind of composition. The simple objects are the ultimate elements of reality. They constitute the substance of the world. They are permanent and unchanging.

But a simple object enters into combinations with other simple objects. These combinations or configurations of simple objects are not, like the objects themselves, fixed and unchanging. They can alter in time, or cease to exist.

A configuration of simple objects is a 'state of affairs' in the world. A possible configuration is a possible state of affairs; an actual configuration is an existing state of affairs.

It is essential to the notion of a simple object that it *can* enter into combinations with other objects, that it can be a constituent of a state of affairs. The *Tractatus* introduces here the notion of *the form* of an object. 'The possibility of its occurring in states of affairs is the form of an object' (*T*, 2.0141). An object can enter into some states of affairs (configurations) and not into others. These possibilities are fixed, unchanging. They lie in the nature of the simple object. The *Tractatus* employs the metaphor of *a space* surrounding an object as an image of the object's possible combinations with other objects. 'Each thing is, as it were, in a space of possible states of affairs' (*T*, 2.013).

We now ascend to a still higher level of abstraction – to 'the form of the world'. We said that each simple object carries with it a space of possibilities. These possibilities are *intrinsic* to the object. To conceive of an object is to conceive of these possibilities. If we now form the conception of *all* objects, we are conceiving of the *totality* of the possible combinations of objects, which is the totality of possible states of affairs, of possible situations in the world. This totality of possibilities is 'the form of the world'. It consists of every possible state of affairs. It is identical with the whole of 'logical space'. The possibilities that *exist* are the facts. The possibilities that do not exist are still possibilities.

The form of the world does not change over time. The realm of what is possible, logically possible, is fixed, unchanging. The form of the world is timeless, eternal. The form of the world is completely a priori. It is prior to all discoveries and inventions, to all experience and all change. (This conception gives one a heady feeling, a sort of dizziness.)

We have centred our attention so far on the conceptions of possibility and reality. We turn now to the theory of *language* of the *Tractatus*. Language just is the totality of propositions (*T*, 4.001). Let us consider again what a 'proposition' is. Any sentence that has sense is a proposition. But also a map, a drawing, a diagram, is a proposition. A sentence that has sense presents (pictures, describes) a possible state of affairs in the world. The sense of a sentence, a proposition, just is the possible situation that it presents (*T*, 2.221).

Among propositions there are 'elementary' ones and non-elementary ones. The elementary propositions are the *basic* propositions. Each non-elementary proposition is constructed out of elementary propositions: It is a 'truth-function' of elementary propositions.

What is the composition of an elementary proposition? It is composed solely of simple signs, called 'names'. The 'simplicity' of a name *consists* in its *meaning* a simple object. 'A name means an object. The object is its meaning' (*T*, 3.203).

The significance of this statement has been much commented on. I think the best clue to understanding it is found in another statement, which is that 'In a proposition a name deputizes for an object' (*T*, 3.22). The idea is that when a name occurs in an elementary sentence, the name 'takes the place of' an object: the name is a substitute, a replacement, for a simple object.

This is a striking conception. A simple object is not a word, nor any other kind of sign. It cannot itself occur in a sentence. But a sentence can contain a sign that 'takes the place of', 'deputizes for', 'acts for', a simple object. The sign, called 'a name', will have all of the *powers* that the object has for which it deputizes, but these powers belong to the name in the medium of language, not in the medium of reality. In a sense a name is a 'duplicate' of the object for which it deputizes. But it is a duplicate in a different medium. The possibilities that a particular simple object has of combining with other objects in states of affairs are duplicated by the possibilities that a name has for combining with other names in elementary sentences.

In an elementary sentence (proposition), one name deputizes for one simple object, another for another and so on. The names are arranged, linked together, in such a way that the proposition, as a whole, is a picture of a possible state of affairs in the world. It depicts the simple objects as related to one another in the *same* way as the names are related to one another in the proposition (*T*, 2.15). Since every proposition is a truth-function of elementary propositions (elementary propositions being truth-functions of themselves), it follows that what every proposition does is the same. Each proposition depicts a possible configuration of simple objects in logical space. If the objects actually are configured in the way that the proposition says they are, then the proposition is true – otherwise false. But even when a proposition is false it has the same 'logical form' as does the possible situation it depicts: for the names in the proposition have the same possibilities of combination as do the corresponding simple objects.

To say anything meaningful, whether true or false, is to depict some possibility or other in that totality of possibilities that constitutes the form of the world. This form is unchanging. Therefore, what *can be said*, and what *can be thought*, is unchanging. The possible configurations of simple objects fix the boundaries of both language and thought.

We have spoken of the conceptions of possibility, reality and language. Let us consider now what a 'thought' is. A thought, like a proposition, is a *picture*. Like any picture it presents a possible situation in logical space (*T*, 2.202). But a thought cannot be simply identified with a 'proposition' – with a meaningful sentence. In an exchange of letters between Russell and Wittgenstein in August 1919, Russell asked: 'What are the constituents of a thought?' Wittgenstein replied: 'I don't know *what* the constituents of a thought are, but I know *that* it must have such constituents which correspond to the words of language' (*NB*, 'Appendix', p. 130). To Russell's further question, 'Does a *Gedanke* [thought] consist of words?', Wittgenstein replied: 'No! But of psychical constituents that have the same sort of relation to reality as words. What those constituents are I don't know' (ibid., p. 131). Notice that Wittgenstein said, without any qualification, that thoughts are composed of 'psychical constituents', i.e. mental elements. The straightforward interpretation of his remarks is that *all* thoughts are composed of mental elements. *No* thought consists of words, spoken or written. Of course the *Tractatus* holds that a thought can be *expressed* in physical signs. 'In a sentence a thought [*Gedanke*] is expressed in a way that is perceptible to the senses' (*T*, 3.1). But a thought does not *have* to be expressed in a physical sentence. Since a thought is a picture, it must be a configuration of elements which depicts a possible state of affairs. That is the *sense* of the thought.

A thought is a structure with a sense. A meaningful sentence is also a structure with a sense. The view of the *Tractatus* would seem to be that when a thought is expressed in a sentence, what happens is that the sense of the thought is *thought into* the sentence. The physical sentence is given the same sense that the thought already has. Thus, there are two structures with the same sense. One structure is composed of mental elements, the other of words. Since these two structures have the same sense, they can be regarded as one and the same 'proposition'. [2]

According to the *Tractatus* there is a hierarchy of ordered structures. A state of affairs in the world is a structure of simple objects. A thought is a structure of mental elements. A proposition of language is a structure of signs. If a particular proposition is *true* there are three structures which, in a sense, are equivalent. There is a configuration of simple objects which *constitutes* a state of affairs. There is a configuration of mental elements which *depicts* that state of affairs. There is a configuration of signs, which also depicts that state of affairs. These are three parallel structures in the three different domains of reality, thought and language. Two of these structures are pictures of the other one.

An important feature of the notion of picturing is that a picture and what it depicts must have the same number of elements. 'In a proposition there must be exactly as much to be distinguished as in the situation that it presents. The two must possess the same logical (mathematical) multiplicity' (*T*, 4.04). This implies that if a proposition is a true picture of an existing state of affairs, then the proposition and the state of affairs must each have the same number of elements. And a thought too must have exactly the same number of elements as does the situation in the world that it depicts. Wittgenstein, in the *Philosophical Investigations*, gives precisely this account of his previous conception in the *Tractatus*: 'These concepts: proposition, language, thought, world, stand in line one behind the other, each equivalent to each' (*PI*, 96). This grand design was what the intellectual world had been waiting for. It explained how a thought, whether or not it was expressed in words, could depict external reality. A thought does this by virtue of being a *model* of the reality it depicts. A thought is a picture; and 'A picture is a model of reality' (*T*, 2.12). The conception of the *Tractatus* explained how one could *say* something. The sentence one utters, just like the thought it expresses, will be a model of the situation that is being described. Both a proposition and a thought *reproduce*, in a sense, the situation they describe.

A thought is composed of mental elements, a sentence of words, reality of simple objects. How can these three domains, composed of such different elements, have anything in common? But they do have something in common. They are *isomorphic*. This is what binds them together. This is how thought and sentence can be pictures, models, of a situation in the world. The three are different; yet in a sense they are the same. If the proposition you state is *true*, then your word-proposition, the thought it expresses, and the situation in the world that they describe, are all identical in structure.

33

CRITICISM OF THE *TRACTATUS*

Many sentences of our ordinary speech do not seem to be 'pictures' or 'models' of what they describe. 'She apologized for the badly cooked roast', is a description of something that happened. Perhaps, in a loose sense, it might be called a 'picture' of what happened. But is it a picture in the precise sense of the *Tractatus*? Is there an 'isomorphism' between that sentence and what happened? We hardly know what to think. The *Tractatus* acknowledges that 'At first sight a sentence – one set out on the printed page, for example – does not seem to be a picture of the reality with which it is concerned' (*T*, 4.011). But Wittgenstein went on to insist that, despite this superficial appearance, these sentences do *prove* to be pictures (ibid.).

How would this be proved? By a process of *analysis*. If the statement about the lady who apologized is not itself an 'elementary' proposition, then it can be analysed until it appears as a truth-function of elementary propositions, which consist only of simple signs, i.e. names. The names deputize for the simple objects that compose the described situation. This situation will be displayed as a configuration of simple objects. When all of this is done the arrangement of names will match the arrangement of simple objects. The complete analysis of what a sentence *meant* will result in an exact correlation between simple signs and simple objects. The true sense of a proposition is displayed when it is analysed into elementary propositions containing a specific and countable number of simple signs.

But does anyone have a mastery of this supposed procedure of analysis? Wittgenstein later realized that *he* did not – and if he did not then surely no one else did. In remarks probably written in 1936, he admitted that he did not even have a method for determining whether a given proposition was or was not an elementary proposition:

> If you want to use the appellation 'elementary proposition' as I did in the *Tractatus Logico-Philosophicus*, and as Russell used 'atomic proposition', you may call the sentence 'Here there is a red rose' an elementary proposition. That is to say, it doesn't contain a truth-function and it isn't defined by an expression which contains one. But if we're to say that a proposition isn't an elementary proposition unless its complete logical analysis shows that it isn't built out of other propositions by truth-functions, we are presupposing that we have an idea of what

such an 'analysis' would be. Formerly, I myself spoke of a 'complete analysis', and I used to believe that philosophy had to give a definitive dissection of propositions so as to set out clearly all their connections and remove all possibilities of misunderstanding. I spoke as if there was a calculus in which such a dissection would be possible. I vaguely had in mind something like the definition that Russell had given for the definite article, and I used to think that in a similar way one would be able to use visual impressions, etc., to define the concept say of a sphere, and thus exhibit once and for all the connections between the concepts and lay bare the source of all misunderstandings, etc. At the root of all this there was a false and idealized picture of the use of language.

(PG, p. 211)

The thesis of the *Tractatus* that every genuine proposition is a 'picture' presupposed that there is at hand a calculus, a deductive procedure, by which logical analysis can determine whether any proposition whatever is an elementary proposition or is a truth-function of elementary propositions. The realization that the notion of there being an available calculus in which a 'complete analysis' could be carried out was an *illusion*, meant that a basic assumption of the picture-theory of propositions was undermined. The once powerful idea that every meaningful sentence is a picture was now seen not to have a clear meaning. This was a severe setback for the theory of language in the *Tractatus*.

SIMPLE OBJECTS

An age-old conception of metaphysical philosophy, a conception that continued into the twentieth century, is that reality is composed of simple elements. The world is full of complex things and events: but these are composed of non-complex, simple, things – which, in Russell's phrase, are 'the ultimate furniture of the world'. To many minds it has seemed obvious that reality must be composed of simple elements. Leibniz maintained that there must be simple substances because there are compounds. The *Tractatus* did not rely on anything so elusive as obviousness: it undertook to prove that *language* would be impossible if reality was not composed of simple elements.

Why does language require that reality be composed of simple objects? This is a difficult point to grasp. But it is clear that Wittgenstein thought that if reality were *not* composed of simple objects, then no sentence, no proposition, would have a *definite sense*. The *Notebooks* say: 'The requirement of simple things *is* the requirement for the definiteness of sense' (*NB*, p. 63). The *Tractatus* says: 'The requirement that simple signs be possible is the requirement that sense be definite' (*T*, 3.23). These two remarks come to the same. For 'simple signs' and 'simple things' are interlocking concepts. To prove that either is required is to prove that both are required.

There is an argument in the *Tractatus* to prove that the things (the objects) to which the words of language ultimately refer must be *simple*: otherwise the sentence we speak would not have *sense*. The following series of statements occurs:

Objects are simple.

(*T*, 2.02)

Objects constitute the substance of the world.

(*T*, 2.021)

If the world had no substance, then whether a proposition had sense would depend on whether another proposition was true.

(*T*, 2.0211)

It would then be impossible to frame any picture of the world (true or false).

(*T*, 2.0212)

The assumption here is that the things which the words of language designate or signify must be either simple or complex. If there were no simple things, then words would designate only complex things. But a complex thing, since it is composed of parts or elements, can come apart or be destroyed. A complex thing can cease to exist. So if the words of a sentence designated only complex things, and those complex things no longer existed, then the words would not designate anything at all, and so the sentence would not have any sense. In order for it to be guaranteed that the sentence does have sense, it would have to be *true* that those complexes do exist. Suppose a proposition, *P*, states that certain complex things are related to one another in such-and-such a way. Another proposition, *Q*, states that those complex things referred to by *P*, do exist. Unless *Q* is true, *P* is meaningless. Therefore, whether *P* has sense depends on whether *Q* is true.

If Q were true it would be only *contingently* true. Whether P had sense would depend on a contingent matter of fact. From the viewpoint of the *Tractatus*, this would be intolerable.

Furthermore, an infinite regress would exist. For the proposition, Q, which by virtue of being true guarantees the sense of P, would itself refer to complex things, that might or might not exist. So whether Q had sense would depend on whether another proposition, R, was true. The same for R – and so on, without end.

The endless regress would mean that no proposition whatever had a fixed, stable sense. Thus it would be impossible to frame any picture of any state of affairs. Language would contain no descriptions, either true or false, of situations in the world.

The foregoing reasoning is an attempt to prove that the objects to which words ultimately refer must be simple things – for if they were complex, language would be impossible.

There seems to be another line of reasoning in the *Tractatus* not set out so explicitly, but closely related to the above argument. The *Tractatus* says: 'A proposition has one and only one complete analysis' (*T*, 3.25). This certainly implies that the analysis of any proposition must be able to be *completed*. We saw from the quoted passage in the *Philosophical Grammar* that Wittgenstein later realized that he did not have in his grasp a procedure of analysis that could produce a final analysis of every proposition. But in the *Tractatus* he seems to have thought that no analysis could be completed *unless* the ultimate constituents of reality were *simple* things. A complex thing, to be fully understood, would have to be analysed into its constituent elements and the relationships between them. But if those elements were themselves *complex*, then the analysis could not stop there. It would have to go on and on, never terminating, since it would always be arriving at complex things which themselves had to be analysed into *their* constituent parts. Analysis could never display the final and complete sense of a proposition. A proposition would not *have* a final, determinate sense. One could never arrive at a point where one could say: '*This* is the sense of the proposition.' No proposition would depict a definite state of affairs in the world. In asserting a proposition you would not know exactly what you were saying – nor would anyone else. So for any proposition to have an exact sense, that proposition must be analysable into elementary propositions, composed of signs that deputize for simple objects. There must be simple objects in order for the sentences we utter to have a definite sense.

The *Tractatus* says: 'It is obvious that the analysis of propositions must bring us to elementary propositions which consist of names in immediate combination' (*T*, 4.221). There is nothing vague about a simple object; it has a fixed unchanging nature. Two objects can either combine with one another – or they cannot. Each object has a specific 'form', which consists of its possible combinations with other objects in states of affairs. Simple signs of language ('names') deputize for these simple elements of reality. Names are combined in an elementary sentence in such a way that the sentence depicts a possible configuration of the corresponding elements of reality. A possible configuration of simple elements is something absolutely precise; either it exists in reality or it does not exist. The sense of the sentence that describes this possibility will be equally precise. In this way, the demand for definiteness of sense in *all* propositions is satisfied: for each non-elementary proposition is simply a truth-function of elementary propositions.

This elegant and eminently satisfying vision of the perfect order holding between language and reality was struck a crushing blow by the *Investigations*. Paragraphs 47 through 49 present a *tour de force* in philosophical criticism. What is attacked is the assumption of the *Tractatus* (and of much previous metaphysics) that the distinction between the simple and the complex has an *absolute* sense. In a variety of telling examples Wittgenstein shows very clearly that whether any particular thing is called a 'simple' thing or a 'complex' thing depends on accepted conventions, on decisions made for practical purposes, or on what comparisons are at issue.

Is my visual image of a tree a simple or a complex image? When put like that, one doesn't know what to say. But it might be decided that the image is to be called 'simple' if it is an image only of a tree trunk, but 'complex' if it is an image of trunk and branches. But also the image of the trunk and branches of a tree might be called a 'simple' image, in contrast with the image of that tree together with a house and a telephone pole. Any particular thing can be regarded either as 'simple' or as 'complex', depending on what contrasts are at stake. Nothing is 'intrinsically' simple, or complex. Is marriage a simple relationship, or a complex one? Considered apart from all circumstances, the question has no meaning. But if the characters, temperaments, interests, of the married people are taken into account, then we might wish to say that *some* marriages are simple relationships and others complex ones.

The 'objects' of the *Tractatus* were deemed to be intrinsically simple.[3] But since nothing whatever is 'intrinsically' simple, simple in an 'absolute' sense, then this basic conception of the *Tractatus* is *empty*; and so is the conception of a 'name' – for a name is supposed to *mean* a simple object; and so is the conception of an 'elementary' proposition – for an elementary proposition is supposed to consist of an interconnection of names; and so is the conception of 'analysis' in the *Tractatus* – for analysis is supposed to determine whether any given proposition is elementary or non-elementary. The impressive edifice of the *Tractatus* is demolished by Wittgenstein's description in the *Investigations* of how the terms 'simple' and 'complex' are *actually used*. This is an example of where one might want to accuse Wittgenstein of destroying everything 'great and important', and where his reply would be that he is destroying nothing but 'air castles' (*Luftgebäude*) (*PI*, 118).

NOTES

1 Wittgenstein, 'A lecture on freedom of the will', notes taken by Yorick Smythies, Cambridge 1946–7, *Philosophical Investigations*, April 1989. My summary is of remarks on pp. 85–7.

2 I argue in greater detail for this interpretation of 'thought' in the *Tractatus* in Norman Malcolm, *Nothing is Hidden*, Oxford, Blackwell, 1986, chapter 4, published in paperback under the title *Wittgenstein: Nothing is Hidden*, Oxford, Blackwell, 1988.

3 Some commentators have been in doubt about this. In my *Nothing is Hidden*, chapter 3, I argue that the objects of the *Tractatus* must be understood to be 'simple' in an absolute sense, apart from all human decisions and comparisons.

3

THE ESSENCE
OF LANGUAGE

When Wittgenstein, in the *Investigations*, brought to light the fluid character of the distinction between the simple and the complex, this was fatal to the theory of reality, language and thought of the *Tractatus*. But the *Tractatus* is only one book, *one* attempt to capture these fundamental concepts in the net of philosophical analysis. One failed attempt cannot prove that the ancient goal of philosophical analysis is impossible to attain.

But another development in the *Investigations*, one of its main themes, does show this to be an impossible goal. The aim of philosophical analysis, when considered at the highest level of abstraction, was to reveal the essential nature of *language*, of the sentences (propositions) we utter, of what it is to *say* something. Wittgenstein wrote in the *Tractatus Notebooks*: 'My *whole* task consists in explaining the nature of propositions' (*NB*, p. 39). Of the fundamental propositions, the elementary ones, he said: 'As I conceive, e.g., the elementary propositions, there must be something common to them; otherwise I could not speak of all of them collectively as the "elementary propositions"' (*NB*, p. 90). In the *Tractatus* he thought that he had uncovered the essential nature, not just of elementary propositions, but of *all* propositions. He called this 'the general propositional form'. 'The general propositional form is the essence of propositions' (*T*, 5.471). 'To give the essence of propositions means to give the essence of all description, and thus the essence of the world' (*T*, 5.4711). The *Tractatus* actually declares what the general propositional form is:

It now seems possible to give the most general propositional form: that is, to give a description of the propositions of *any* sign-language *whatsoever*. . . . The existence of a general propositional form is proved by the fact that there cannot be a proposition whose form could not have been foreseen (i.e. constructed). The general form of propositions is: This is how things are.

(T, 4.5)

It is a curious idea that the essential nature of language, and of all description, is captured by the words, 'This is how things are.' These words do form a sentence, but how is this sentence actually *used*? If a man uttered this sentence, by itself, he would not have said anything with which one could agree or disagree. He would not have *described* anything. This sentence is in fact employed as a prelude to, or a summation of, informative remarks. Suppose someone said to you, 'How are you getting along?' you might reply: 'Well, this is how things are: My wife is ill and cannot take care of the children. I cannot take care of them because I have to go to my job. We are in a dreadful situation!' As Wittgenstein observes in the *Investigations*, to say that the mere statement, 'This is how things are', agrees or does not agree with reality would be 'obvious nonsense' (*PI*, 134). The words that are supposed to disclose the essential nature of propositions and of descriptions, are themselves neither a proposition nor a description.

But the main interest of the quoted passages of the *Tractatus* lies elsewhere, namely, in the assumption that there is, and must be, an essential nature of language. In his later thinking Wittgenstein repudiated this assumption. It pertains to 'the great question' to which he addresses himself as follows:

Here we come up against the great question which lies behind all these considerations. – For someone might object against me: 'You take the easy way out! You talk about all sorts of language games, but have nowhere said what the essence of a language game, and hence of language, is: what is common to all these activities, and what makes them into language or parts of language. So you let yourself off the very part of the investigation that once gave you yourself most headache, the part about the *general form of propositions* and of language.'

And this is true. – Instead of producing something common to all that we call language, I am saying that these phenomena have no one thing in common which makes us use the same word for all, – but that they are *related* to one another in many different ways. And it is because of this relationship, or these relationships, that we call them all 'language'.

(*PI*, 65)

The fact that many phenomena are referred to by one name exerts on us a compulsion to assume that these phenomena must have something in common which is their essential nature. A good illustration of this is the following. The historian, Sir Herbert Butterfield, writing on the subject of military battles in his book *Man on His Past*, says that 'every battle in world history may be different from every other battle, but they must have something in common if we can group them under the term "battle" at all'.[1] Notice the striking similarity between Butterfield's assumption and the assumption of Wittgenstein in the *Notebooks* that in regard to the 'elementary propositions', 'there must be something common to them; otherwise I could not speak of all of them collectively as the "elementary propositions"' (*NB*, p. 90).

If we reflect on military battles that have occurred in human history we will remember that there have been battles between foot soldiers and foot soldiers, cavalry and foot soldiers, cavalry and cavalry. Battles between ships and ships, ships and land fortresses, ships and aircraft, aircraft and aircraft, tanks and infantry, tanks and tanks, aircraft and tanks. Battles have lasted for a few hours, or for months or years. Battles have been fought in small fields, or in areas of hundreds of square miles. Weapons of battle have been fists, clubs, pitchforks, knives, swords, axes, spears, cross-bows, pistols, rifles, machine guns, cannon, bombs. Some battles have ended in victory of one side, others in a draw. In some battles the combatants have fought hand to hand, in others at a distance of twenty miles. Battles involve fighting; but what is common to these various forms of fighting? And there is fighting other than in military battles, as in boxing matches, family quarrels, court cases, business mergers, football games. The use of the one word 'battle' charms us into thinking that there must be something in common to all battles, something that justifies the application of the same word. But as Wittgenstein says: 'Don't think, but look' (*PI*, 66). And when we do look we do not see a common nature of battles, any more than we see something that is common to all of the things that are called 'games'.

Philosophy has worked hard for many centuries, trying to reveal the essential nature not only of language, but of justice, beauty, art, morality, causality, intentional action, knowledge, understanding, memory and so on. This was the accepted mission of philosophy. An investigation of the concept of causality would be an attempt to analyse the concept, to take it apart, as it were; to determine what are the necessary and sufficient conditions for its being the case that something, A, *caused* something, B. An attempt to specify these conditions would be a *theory* of causality – an *explanation* of the nature of 'the causal relation'.

After his return to philosophical research, Wittgenstein came to the realization that 'what we call "proposition" and "language" is not the formal unity that I had imagined, but is a family of structures more or less related to one another' (*PI*, 108). The implication of this perception was that there *could not be* a correct philosophical theory of language. If the concept of language is not a unitary concept, we should expect the same of the other concepts with which philosophy has struggled. If the word 'cause', as it is actually used, does not have a uniform employment, but an irregular one, then there cannot be a correct theory of the essence of causation – since there is no essence of causation. The same holds for the concepts of *truth, representation, knowledge, justice, the good* and so on. Wittgenstein's new insight into the actual working of language implies that the enterprise of philosophical analysis, as traditionally conceived, is based on a false assumption.

This does not mean that there is no work left for philosophy. It does mean that its role should be differently understood and practised. That there are philosophical confusions is a fact of life. A worthwhile enterprise is to try to *disentangle* these confusions. One may be perplexed, for example, as to whether the *motive* of a human act is the *cause* of the act. Not everyone feels this perplexity – but some do, and it is uncomfortable. An investigation into some of the ways in which the words 'motive' and 'cause' are used will show important differences in their use. This kind of investigation may be called 'philosophical analysis', if one likes – but it is not 'analysis' in the full-blown sense of the tradition. It does not search for *definitions* of the concepts of *cause* and *motive*, but only for similarities and differences between them. But the emphasis is on *differences*.

In 1948 Drury once asked Wittgenstein what he thought of Hegel's philosophy. Wittgenstein replied:

"Hegel seems to me to be always wanting to say that things which look different are really the same. Whereas my interest is in showing that things which look the same are really different. I was thinking of using as a motto for my book a quotation from *King Lear*: 'I'll teach you differences.' " Then laughing: "The remark 'You'd be surprised' wouldn't be a bad motto either."

(*R*, p. 171)

NOTICING DIFFERENCES

'You'd be surprised' would indeed be a fitting motto for the *Philosophical Investigations*. That is exactly what happens when an unexpected difference comes to light. One is surprised: it isn't what one would have thought – even though it is in *one's own familiar language* that the differences are shown! Even more than by differences in the use of different words, we are surprised by differences in the way in which the *same* word is used in different contexts.

At this stage in my discussion it might be helpful to provide an illustration. Let us consider the word 'belief'. Many philosophers have assumed that when a person believes something, the belief is a 'state', or even a 'mental state', of that person. Is this correct?

When we are inquiring about a *state* of something, we can ask, 'When did it begin and end; how long did it last?' When water in a pan over a fire begins to boil, that is a change in the state of the water. We can ask 'When did it begin boiling?', 'How long has it been boiling?' The state of boiling has a beginning and an ending. The period of time between the beginning and ending is the duration of the boiling. So at least in one common use of the word 'state', a state of something has *duration*. When a philosopher asserts that a person's belief is a 'state', or a 'mental state', of the person, he is probably supposing that a belief has some duration. In order to see how much truth there is in that assumption, let us look at the following examples:

1 A merchant believes that his clerk is stealing money from him. The merchant came to this belief one week ago, when he noticed that money was missing from the till. But this belief in the clerk's guilt came to an end today, when the merchant discovered that a member of his own family was the one who had been robbing the till. This belief in the clerk's guilt was a state of one week's duration.

44

2 A man sits on a chair and it collapses. Afterward he says: 'When I sat down on the chair, of course I believed it would hold me. I had no thought of the possibility of its collapsing' (*PI*, 575). Would it make sense here to ask, 'When did you begin to have that belief?' The man had no attitude towards the chair and no thoughts about it – until it collapsed. It would make no sense to assign a duration to his belief that the chair would hold him. This belief was not a state.

3 I am about to sit on a chair, but become suspicious of it. I test it and it seems quite solid. I say, 'I believe it will hold me', and I sit on it. I did think of the possibility of its collapsing, but concluded after testing it that it would hold me. Ten minutes later it collapsed. One could say that my belief came into existence when I drew that conclusion, and came to an end when the chair collapsed. In this example my belief was a state of ten minutes' duration.

4 A man is distressed by information indicating that a close friend of his is untrustworthy. He *wants* to believe in the integrity of his friend. Later he says, 'In spite of everything he did, I held fast to my belief in his integrity.' Wittgenstein's comment on this case is: 'Here there is thought, and perhaps a constant struggle to maintain an attitude' (*PI*, 575).

5 Expectation is connected with belief. Suppose I received a letter from someone who announced that he would visit me in a week's time. From the time of reading the letter until his arrival I expected him. But my mind was not *occupied* with his coming. I did not have fearful or anxious or joyful thoughts about his coming. I did not *think* about it at all. Yet it is true that during that week I believed he would come. This belief or expectation was a state of one week's duration.

But was it a 'mental state' or 'state of mind'? Consider the following remarks by Wittgenstein:

> We say 'I expect him', when we believe he will come, though his coming does not *occupy our thoughts*. (Here 'I expect him' means 'I should be surprised if he didn't come' – and that will not be called a description of a state of mind.) But we also say 'I expect him', when this means: I am eagerly awaiting him.
>
> (*PI*, 577)

When I am impatiently awaiting him, when my mind is filled with joyful thoughts of his coming – this is a state of mind. But 'I should be surprised if he didn't come' is not a description of a state of mind.

Here is another example of expectation and belief:

6 'I watch a burning fuse, in high excitement follow the advance of the flame and its approach to the explosive. Perhaps I don't think of anything at all, or have a multitude of disconnected thoughts. This is certainly a case of expecting.'

(*PI*, 576)

If I said, 'I was filled with dread as I waited for the explosion', that would be a description of a state of mind.

What is the philosophical significance of these examples? They show that the word 'belief' has different meanings in different contexts. Many philosophers have assumed that a belief (*any* belief) is a mental state or state of mind. Our survey of a few cases shows that this assumption is false.

The belief in case (1) is a state; but it would not be a mental state or state of mind – unless (for example) the merchant was obsessed with feelings of outrage about the clerk's supposed thievery. In (2) the belief was not even a state, and therefore not a mental state. In (3) the belief was a state. But after I tested the chair I had no more anxious thoughts, nor any thoughts at all about the chair – until it collapsed. The words 'I believed it would hold me' would *not*, in case (3), be a description of a state of mind. In (4) the words, 'In spite of everything he did, I held fast to a belief in his integrity', might describe a state of mind – a painful struggle to hold fast to his trust in his friend. In (5) the belief is a state but, as Wittgenstein says, not a state of mind. In (6) the person expects an explosion (and of course *believes* there will be one). 'I watched the progress of the burning fuse with growing dread', would certainly be a description of a state of mind.

One could give more, and different, examples of how the words 'belief' and 'believe' are actually used. But probably these few examples are enough to make the point – which is that the word 'belief' means different things in different situations. Sometimes, but not always, a belief is a state. Sometimes, but not always, a belief is a mental state or state of mind. There is no such thing as *the* meaning of the word 'belief'. A philosophical theory about *the meaning* of the word 'belief' – an attempt to give an analytic definition of the concept of belief – is bound to be a non-starter.

It is possible for there to be two different attitudes toward these examples of belief. One attitude is to feel frustrated by the variety found in them. We may say to ourselves: 'We have not yet discovered the true nature of belief. It must be something that is concealed in these differences.'

Another attitude is to say: 'The assumption that the word "belief" has a unitary meaning is not justified. We look and don't find it – because it isn't there. Nothing is concealed.'

In *Zettel* Wittgenstein makes some observations about the word 'thinking', that apply equally well to the word 'belief':

> It is not to be expected of this word that it should have a unified employment; instead the opposite should be expected.
>
> (*Z*, 112)

> And the naive idea that one forms of it does not correspond to reality at all. We expect a smooth, regular contour and what we manage to see is ragged. Here it might really be said that we have constructed a false picture.
>
> (*Z*, 111)

The irregularity, the 'raggedness', that confronts us in the use of the word 'belief' is how it actually *is*. There is no unity *behind* the irregularity. In his 'grammatical investigations', Wittgenstein shows how the words 'understand', 'know', 'think', 'mean' and so on, alter their sense from context to context. This does not satisfy our expectation of 'a smooth, regular contour'. But it may *free us* from that expectation.

NOTE

1 Quoted by John Keegan, *The Face of Battle*, Harmondsworth, Penguin, 1978, p. 302.

4

UNDERLYING
MECHANISMS

One might suppose that within a few years after the publication of the *Philosophical Investigations*, the direction of philosophical work would have sharply altered. Philosophers would no longer be searching for the universal, the essential. But if one supposed this, one would be wrong. Books containing *theories* of art, of thinking, of belief, of ethics, of action, of knowledge, of language, continue to abound. Much of this writing, of course, has gone down without leaving a ripple; but some of it has made waves.

The books of Noam Chomsky are prominent in the latter group. He has had, and apparently continues to have, a marked influence on psychology, linguistics, semantics and philosophy of mind. His writings include the following: *Aspects of the Theory of Syntax*, *Cartesian Linguistics* and *Language and Mind*.[1] One striking feature of Chomsky's views about language is that they have a strong resemblance to the conceptions of the *Tractatus* (published with English translation in 1922); and a second striking feature is that they seem to *totally ignore* the devastating criticism of those conceptions in the *Philosophical Investigations* (published with English translation in 1951).

In his writings Chomsky calls attention to several important characteristics of the normal use of language. It is innovative; it is 'potentially infinite' in scope (i.e. unlimited or unbounded); it is not controlled by detectable stimuli; it is generally appropriate to the situations in which it is spoken (L&M, pp. 11–12). Another impressive fact is the great disparity between the meagre data a child is presented with when learning language, and the extent of the

48

competence in language which the child eventually develops. Chomsky puts this point in the following way:

> The native speaker has acquired a grammar on the basis of very restricted and degenerate evidence; the grammar has empirical consequences that extend far beyond the evidence.
>
> (L&M, p. 27)

> We cannot avoid being struck by the enormous disparity between knowledge and experience – in the case of language, between the generative grammar that expresses the linguistic competence of the native speaker and the meagre and degenerate data on the basis of which he has constructed this grammar for himself.
>
> (L&M, p. 78)

There is indeed a remarkable disparity – a gap – between the scanty input of instruction and the few examples that are presented to the learner, and the rich mastery of language that eventually blossoms. Chomsky's problem is how to account for this disparity. The linguistic reach of any normal speaker surpasses by far what he has been explicitly taught, or has picked up from his linguistic environment. Chomsky's view is that we must postulate the existence of something that will *fill* this gap. Looked at from the viewpoint of *causation*, this could be regarded as an application of the Cartesian principle that there cannot be 'more reality' in an effect than in its cause. Chomsky says:

> The problem raised is that of specifying the mechanisms that operate on the data of sense and produce knowledge of language – linguistic competence. It is obvious that such mechanisms exist.
>
> (L&M, p. 22)

> We must recognize that even the most familiar phenomena require explanation and that we have no privileged access to the underlying mechanisms, no more so than in physiology or physics.
>
> (L&M, p. 26)

Chomsky thinks that the only plausible theory of this gap-filling mechanism is the postulating of a structure that is *innate* in every human being.

> We must postulate an innate structure that is rich enough to account for the disparity between experience and knowledge, one that can account for the construction of the empirically justified generative grammars within the given limitations of time and access to data.
>
> (*L&M*, p. 79)

The innate structure that Chomsky postulates is 'the general theory of language' – also called by him 'universal grammar'.

> Suppose we assign to the mind, as an innate property, the general theory of language that we have called 'universal grammar'. . . . The theory of universal grammar, then, provides a schema to which any particular grammar must conform. Suppose, furthermore, that we can make this schema sufficiently restrictive so that very few possible grammars conforming to the schema will be consistent with the meagre and degenerate data actually available to the language learner. His task, then, is to search among the possible grammars and select one that is not definitely rejected by the data available to him.
>
> (*L&M*, p. 88)

Chomsky holds that there is 'a general theory of language' which embodies 'the necessary and sufficient conditions that a system must meet in order to qualify as a potential human language' (*L&M*, p. 88).

Here we see a conspicuous similarity between Chomsky's thinking, and the thinking of Wittgenstein in the *Tractatus*. Both subscribe to an essentialist theory of language. According to the *Tractatus* there is 'a general form of propositions' which expresses the essential nature of all propositions; and since language just *is* the totality of propositions, the general form of propositions is the essence of language. The *Tractatus* holds that 'there cannot be a proposition whose form could not have been foreseen' (*T*, 4.5). So there cannot be a language whose form could not have been foreseen. The same is true of Chomsky's view: if there is a 'universal grammar', then there cannot be a form of language that could not have been anticipated.

There is, however, nothing in the *Tractatus* that corresponds to Chomsky's notion of how a language learner acquires his first natural language, i.e. the language of the community in which he grows up. This learner, according to Chomsky, is already in possession of 'the theory of universal grammar', which was not acquired through experience, but is innate. Armed with this theory of all possible languages, the learner picks out the particular language that best accords with the input from his linguistic community. In his *Aspects of the Theory of Syntax* Chomsky describes language-learning as follows:

> To acquire language, a child must devise a hypothesis compatible with the presented data – he must select from the store of potential grammars a specific one that is appropriate to the data available to him.
>
> (*Aspects*, p. 36)

> The child approaches the data with the presumption that they are drawn from a language of a certain antecedently well-defined type, his problem being to determine which of the (humanly) possible languages is that of the community in which he is placed. Language learning would be impossible unless this were the case.
>
> (*Aspects*, p. 27)

According to Chomsky's theory every normal human child would have to be a *prodigy* right from the start! Fairly soon after birth a human infant begins to be bombarded by utterances, issuing from adoring parents and admiring visitors. This little marvel, according to Chomsky, 'approaches the data with the presumption that they are drawn from a language of a certain antecedently well-defined type'.

But it *makes no sense* to attribute this 'presumption' to a small child; nor to suppose that a child has in his possession a 'general theory of language' – a highly abstract theory of the necessary and sufficient conditions that any possible language must meet.

Let us just suppose that there was a child who did *not* have in his grasp the general theory of language, and who did *not* 'devise a hypothesis compatible with the presented data'. Let us further suppose that this child, despite his handicap, *did* gradually learn the language of his community – just as other children do. Chomsky would have to say: 'It is impossible that there should be such a child.' But Chomsky could have no empirical grounds for that assertion. Nothing that a child did, a child who does not yet know the use of even one word, could show that this child was in possession of an abstract theory of the form of every possible language. No clinical observations could be evidence that the child had 'devised a hypothesis' that was compatible with the linguistic data which surrounds it. Could Chomsky set up tests on two groups of infants, one group consisting of those infants who have a grasp of the theory of 'universal grammar', and who also devise hypotheses to ascertain which possible natural language is the language of their community, and the other group composed of infants who have no conception of universal grammar and who devise no hypotheses – and could Chomsky discover that only those in the first group actually learn the language of their community? Of course not. Chomsky would have no way of determining whether a given infant belongs to one group or the other.

In his last writing, *On Certainty*, Wittgenstein says: 'Language did not emerge from reasoning' (*OC*, 475). This is a striking remark – especially when one compares it with Chomsky's view. According to the latter, a child's mastery of its first natural language is a triumph of reasoning – reasoning that is carried on before the child knows how to *say* anything! This postulated reasoning is something that is visible neither to the observation of adults, nor to the child. It is something that goes on underneath the surface, hidden from everyone.

We come now to a second similarity between the *Tractatus* and Chomsky's conception. According to the *Tractatus* any proposition, any assertion, any statement, is a precise picture of a possible situation in the world.

> A proposition communicates a situation to us, and so it must be *essentially* connected with the situation. And the connection is precisely that it is its logical picture. A proposition states something only in so far as it is a picture.
>
> (*T*, 4.03)

In writing the *Tractatus* Wittgenstein was very worried about the apparent *vagueness* of much of our ordinary language. In the *Notebooks* he says:

> When I say, 'The book is lying on the table', does this really have a completely clear sense? (An *extremely* important question.) But the sense must be clear, for after all we mean *something* by the proposition, and as much as we *certainly* mean must surely be clear.
>
> (*NB*, p. 67)

Is it or is it not possible to talk of a proposition's having a
more or less sharp sense?
It seems clear that what we *mean* must always be 'sharp'.

(*NB*, p. 68)

It is clear that I *know* what I *mean* by the vague sentence.

(*NB*, p. 70)

It is easy to think of cases in which we should be in some doubt as
to whether a book could be rightly said to be 'lying on the table'. It
is lying on some papers that are lying on the table; or one end of the
book is on the table and the other end is propped up by other
books. What we call 'lying on the table' does not have a clear application in all situations. Wittgenstein wanted to insist, nevertheless,
that what I *mean*, in a particular case, must have a perfectly sharp
sense. If a statement of mine did not have, at least for me, an
unambiguous sense, then it would not depict one and only one
situation in the world.

In the *Tractatus* Wittgenstein came to the conclusion that: 'All of
the propositions of our ordinary language are actually in perfect logical
order, just as they are' (*T*, 5.5563). The apparent vagueness of many of
the remarks that people make in daily conversation must be a *misleading* appearance. A truly vague statement would not be in 'perfect logical order'. It would not be a precise depiction of one and only one
situation in the world. It would not have a *definite* sense. Perfect logical
order must be present, even in what looks like a vague sentence, but it
is *concealed*. The *Tractatus* says: 'Language disguises thought. So much
so, that from the outward form of the clothing it is impossible to infer
the form of the thought beneath it' (*T*, 4.002). In Chapter 2 we saw
that, according to the *Tractatus*, the requirement that every statement
have a 'definite' sense could be satisfied only if each statement is
analysable into an array of elementary propositions consisting of
names deputizing for simple objects. This process of analysis would
display the exact sense of a *superficially* vague statement.

This process of analysis cannot be *merely possible*. It must be something that actually goes on when we speak and when we hear others
speak. For we know what we *mean*, and we know what others *mean*.
Rarely, if ever, are we aware of the mental processes of analysis that
we are conducting – or that are taking place in us. The apparently
vague statements of ordinary language are given their actually precise sense by processes of logical analysis that are largely unconscious. The *Tractatus* says: 'Mankind has the ability to construct

languages capable of expressing every sense, without having any idea how each word has meaning or what its meaning is – just as people speak without knowing how the individual sounds are produced' (*T*, 4.002) The conclusion would seem to be that in our daily conversations complicated processes of analysis are occurring, without our awareness of what they are, or even that they occur.

Now this is very similar to Chomsky's conception. For the complex theorizing and hypothesizing that Chomsky attributes to every normal child would not be something of which the child could be aware.

As we saw in Chapter 3, Wittgenstein repudiated his previous assumption that there is an essential nature of language. This was, by implication, a rejection *in advance* of Chomsky's conception of a 'universal grammar'. But Wittgenstein also rejected the notion of the *Tractatus* that apparent vagueness is transformed into actual clarity by rapid processes of logical analysis. This is an example of what he called a *myth*. 'In philosophy one is in constant danger of producing a myth of symbolism, or of mental processes. Instead of simply saying what everyone knows and must admit' (*Z*, 211). But Wittgenstein did not just *call* it a 'myth' and leave it at that. In his careful studies, in his later writings, of examples of one's *understanding* or *meaning* something, of obeying an order, of following a rule, of knowing what one was about to say or do, and so on – he shows that it *is* a myth. When we actually pay attention to what goes on when we speak and when we respond to the words of others, we find no support for the idea that we are constantly employing theories, hypotheses, computations. In conversation our remarks usually conform to the grammar of the words, without our *thinking* of that grammar.

It is useless for a philosopher to hold that the processes of exact thinking take place at a subterranean, unconscious level – as the *Tractatus* hints when it says that it is impossible to gather immediately from everyday language 'what the logic of language is' (*T*, 4.002) – and as Chomsky implies when he says that one cannot hope to determine 'by introspection' either the underlying abstract representations or the swift mental processes that relate these abstract forms to the spoken words of language (*L&M*, p. 43). It is useless because it *begs the question*. It is a way of protecting an assumption that has been put forward as a *requirement*. As the *Investigations* says, 'The more closely we examine actual language, the sharper becomes the conflict between it and our requirement' (*PI*, 107).

Wittgenstein came to realize that the rapid processes of logical analysis, which were supposed to be transforming the apparently vague and disorderly sentences of ordinary speech into propositions having an exact sense, were indeed a myth. But the abstract reasoning that Chomsky attributes to each human child, in its attempt to discover which of the possible languages is the language of its community, does not even deserve the name of 'myth'. For this reasoning is not something that, as a matter of fact, a child does not engage in. Instead the case is this – that to a child who has as yet no natural language at all, it is simply absurd to attribute abstract theories, hypotheses, computations. Chomsky's view is more on the side of the nonsensical than the mythical.

CHOMSKY ON 'EXPLANATION'

Chomsky assumes that there must be an explanation of how a child acquires the language of the community in which it grows up. Chomsky is rightly impressed by the disparity between the meagreness of the linguistic data that are thrust upon a child, and the richness of the normal use of language which the child eventually acquires. Chomsky says: 'The problem raised is that of specifying the mechanisms that operate on the data of sense and produce knowledge of language – linguistic competence. It is obvious that such mechanisms exist' (*L&M*, p. 22). But the 'mechanisms' actually postulated by Chomsky are not, as we have seen, a *possible* explanation.

I wish to raise the question of whether it is right to assume that an explanation is possible. If Chomsky's 'mechanisms' have to be rejected, are we justified in thinking that there must be *some other* mechanisms that do the trick? Chomsky says: 'We must recognize that even the most familiar phenomena require explanation' (*L&M*, p. 26). Surely there is no more familiar phenomenon than the fact that a child of normal intelligence will learn the language of its community. But why should we think that an explanation of this phenomenon is either required or possible?

Suppose I was travelling in Africa and met a person who, for some reason or other, thought I was French. He is impressed by my ability to speak English, and asks me how it came about that I have such a good command of that language. My reply would be: 'English is my native tongue.' This would be an explanation – *for* that person who asked his question only because he wrongly believed that English was not my native language. Once that error is corrected, he will no longer ask how I learned English. He will not say to me: 'And how did you learn your native tongue?' That is not a possible question for him, or for me, or for anyone else.

Of course there may be better and worse methods of teaching English. Will a child's vocabulary increase more rapidly if it is drilled in the memorizing of new words, or if instead it picks up these words from the reading of interesting stories? The results of these different methods of acquiring vocabulary could be compared, and it might be determined that one method is more effective than the other. It would be a matter for empirical investigation.

But Chomsky's inquiry is not engaged with anything that is empirical or testable. His conjectures are concerned with 'the underlying mechanisms' of language acquisition, regardless of any particular techniques of teaching. At bottom Chomsky is amazed by the fact that *so much* can come from *so little*. His response to this apparent fact is to deny its actuality – just as the *Tractatus* denied that the many apparently vague sentences of ordinary conversation really are vague. Chomsky's task is to cancel the outrageous *imbalance* between two quantities – the 'so little' and the 'so much'. He tries to do it by inventing a new quantity, which will stand in equality with the 'so much'. The new quantity will consist of the 'so little' data to which the learner is exposed – *plus* an abstract system underlying behaviour. In this way Chomsky hopes to bridge the gap between the 'data of sense' and 'linguistic competence'.

The trouble is that Chomsky has not corrected the original imbalance – nor has he explained anything. The conjectured system of abstract structures and processes, supposedly innate in each human being, is not only unobservable; it is also inconceivable. You do not explain a puzzling phenomenon by postulating an impossible explanation.

Chomsky must think that a person's having grown up in an English-speaking community is, at best, only a superficial explanation of this person's knowledge of English. Chomsky wants a *deeper* explanation. But what if the idea that there is a deeper explanation is itself a confusion? Chomsky's proposed solution ('We must postulate an innate structure that is rich enough to account for the disparity between experience and knowledge', *L&M*, p. 79) has a vaguely scientific look. But it isn't 'science' in the sense in which science involves observation, experimentation, testing. Chomsky's position may be better understood if we take his initial perplexity to be *philosophical* and his solution *metaphysical*. The solution is an extravagant proposal:

The child is presented with data, and he must inspect hypotheses (grammars) of a fairly restricted class to determine compatibility with this [*sic*] data. Having selected a grammar of the predetermined class, he will then have command of the language generated by this grammar.

(L&M, p. 159)

This search among possible grammars to find one that fits the presented data is not, as already said, an activity that can be meaningfully ascribed to a child. But even if it could be, it would not suffice. Why not? Because what the child would have selected would be a particular grammar which, according to Chomsky, is 'a system of rules'. 'The person who has acquired knowledge of a language has internalized a system of rules that relates sound and meaning in a particular way' (*L&M*, p. 26). But it is one thing to be provided with a rule, and another thing to apply it in the right way. This is a point that Wittgenstein constantly emphasizes in the *Investigations* and in his other late writings. With a little ingenuity we can think of more than one way of applying a given rule – just as Wittgenstein notes that 'we can think of more than *one* application of an algebraic formula' (*PI*, 146). And in *On Certainty* he says: 'But can it be seen from a rule what circumstances logically exclude a mistake in the employment of rules of calculation? ... What use to us is such a rule? Couldn't we (in turn) go wrong in applying it? (*OC*, 26). So even if it made sense to say that every English speaker has 'internalized' a system of rules, and the *same* system of rules, an explanation would be required for the fact that so many people *apply* these rules *in the same way*. It is characteristic of a metaphysical solution that the solution itself gives rise to an insoluble problem. Chomsky seeks to close a gap – but this is done at the cost of generating a similar gap elsewhere.

If someone explains his proficiency in English by informing us that he grew up in an English-speaking community, this is not a 'superficial' explanation. There is no 'deeper' explanation. This is an example of where explanation has come to an end.

NOTE

1 *Aspects of the Theory of Syntax*, Cambridge, Mass., MIT Press, 1965; *Cartesian Linguistics*, New York, Harper & Row, 1966; *Language and Mind*, enlarged edn, New York, Harcourt Brace Jovanovich, 1972.

5

FAILED EXPLANATIONS

Every normal human being succeeds in mastering a language. In the previous chapter we studied an ingenious but vain attempt to explain how this is done. In the present chapter I will consider a variety of important phenomena of human life, along with the failed attempts to explain them.

TALKING

Deer and cats and rabbits do not talk. Why is this? Wittgenstein criticizes a pseudo-explanation in the following remark:

> It is sometimes said that animals do not talk because they lack the mental capacity. And this means: 'they do not think, and that is why they do not talk.' But: they simply do not talk. Or to put it better: they do not use language – if we except the most primitive forms of language – Commanding, questioning, recounting, chatting, are as much a part of our natural history as walking, eating, drinking, playing.
>
> *(PI, 25)*

To say that lower animals do not talk because they lack the mental capacity, and (by implication) that people talk because they do have the necessary mental capacity – may at first sight give the impression of being an explanation. But this impression disappears when we realize that we do not know how to measure and compare mental capacity with the ability to talk.

The concept of 'natural history', which Wittgenstein introduces here, is a central concept in his thinking. In natural history different species of animals are described in terms of posture, locomotion, habitat, breeding, social organization, feeding – the characteristic sounds they make, the way they play, and so on. Some animals live on the earth, some in the earth, some in trees, some in water. Wittgenstein says that his philosophical observations 'are really remarks on the natural history of human beings' (*PI*, 415). That human beings use language is an outstanding feature of their natural history; but to say this is not to give an *explanation* of why they use language. Do we even understand what an explanation might be?

THINKING

Is there an explanation for the fact that human beings think? Apparently there is an inclination to believe so. Sir Frederick Bartlett, the Cambridge psychologist, once wrote:

> I propose to adopt here the view that thinking is a high-level cognitive form of behaviour, and an achievement effected only at a relatively advanced stage of development when, and because, simpler and more direct methods of dealing with environmental demands have broken down. This is a position foreseen long ago by a few people, that is now coming to be widely accepted in professional psychological circles. [1]

This is a peculiar 'explanation' of why human beings think. Bartlett's remarks, if I understand them rightly, seem to imply that at some period in the past mankind did *not* think. Thinking takes many forms. There is thinking in language. But there is also thinking without words, in actions and activities, such as overcoming obstacles, avoiding danger, satisfying needs. A species of creature that did not think *at all* would be far below the mental level of cats and dogs, and would not be human.

Bartlett's conjecture also seems to imply that when mankind was in its supposed non-thinking condition, it gradually came to realize that thinking would be 'a better method' for dealing with environmental threats and demands, than were its previous 'simpler and more direct methods'. If any such realization had occurred, it would itself be high-level thinking. Thus this explanation of how thinking develops out of non-thinking would appear to be self-contradictory.

Wittgenstein puts a similar question about thinking. He asks whether people think because they have found that thinking pays –

because they expect some advantage from it? (*PI*, 467). He notes that *sometimes* people think because it pays: for example, in building boilers they *calculate* the thickness of the boiler walls instead of deciding this by feel – for then fewer explosions occur (*PI*, 469–70). But such an example does not show that in general people think because it pays. Sometimes men court women because they expect financial advantage from it – but this is not generally so. Wittgenstein asks: What would show *why* men think? – implying that we do not understand this question, in its generality. What can we say, other than that this is the kind of creature man is – this is a trait of his natural history: and *that* is not an explanation.

AGREEMENT IN JUDGMENTS

When children are taught the meanings of words, with scanty explanations and few examples, they largely agree in their subsequent application of those words. This is a familiar fact, yet on reflection it seems surprising. Given the paltry character of the instruction, it seems that they would go on to apply those words differently. But, for the most part, they do not: they go on to apply them *in the same way*!

We saw in Chapter 4 how Chomsky was impressed by the disparity between 'the meagre and degenerate data' with which children are presented in their instruction in a language, and the astonishing competence which they eventually develop. I think I said enough there about the untenability, and even the unintelligibility, of Chomsky's solution. In a sense, Chomsky and Wittgenstein are impressed by the same disparity, although there is a difference in the way they look at it. On Wittgenstein's view the 'disparity' or 'gap' between training and mastery is not an empirical matter but a logical or conceptual one. No matter how much the training were enriched, the *possibility* of a pupil's going on in an unexpected way would not be removed. A further important difference is that Chomsky seeks to bridge the gap with an impossible explanation. Wittgenstein offers no explanation at all, and demolishes each proposed explanation.

The same point emerges when we reflect on the concept of 'following a rule'. A rule is stated, with some illustrations of its application. But then in new situations, differing in certain ways from the circumstances of the original examples, there will be general agreement as to what action *accords* with the rule. Wittgenstein devotes a great deal of attention to this topic, both in *Philosophical Investigations* and *Remarks on the Foundations of Mathematics*. A thing he emphasizes is that any rule, expressed in words or signs, can be understood in a surprising way, by someone who has had the normal training and is of normal intelligence. Wittgenstein's well-known example is of a pupil who has been taught to carry out orders of the form '+n'. So at the order '+1' he has learned to write down the series of natural numbers; and has carried out exercises up to 1000. Now he is asked to carry out the order '+2', and he writes 1000, 1004, 1008, 1012. When the instructor objects, the pupil replies: 'But I went on in the same way.' Wittgenstein's comment is:

> It would now be no use to say: 'But can't you see ... ? – and repeat the old examples and explanations. – In such a case we might perhaps say: It is natural for this person to understand our order with our explanations, as *we* would understand the order: 'Add 2 up to 1000, 4 up to 2000, 6 up to 3000, and so on.'
>
> (*PI*, 185)

Consider another example. An instructor has written down the initial segment of a series, e.g. 1, 7, 14, 22. . . . He tells his pupil to continue the series. Instead of writing 31 after 22, the pupil writes 43. The instructor says 'That's wrong. You did not continue in the same way.' The pupil protests: 'But I did continue in the say way. The difference between 1 and 22 in the initial segment is 21; and the difference between 22 and 43 is also 21. So I did go on in the same way.' The pupil took the initial segment as *one unit*, and the segment 22, 43 as the *second unit* of the series. He continued the series in a way that the instructor had not anticipated. The instructor says that the pupil is wrong – but he can hardly claim that the pupil was being unreasonable.

There is a temptation to think that what is required for following a rule is that one should *interpret* the rule correctly. What is to be understood here by 'interpretation'? If by 'interpreting' the rule correctly, one just means *following* it – then nothing has been explained. If, however, by an 'interpretation' one means another *formulation* of the rule, in different words or signs, then we have got no further: the same problem as with the original formulation repeats itself.

This perplexity about how one can follow a rule gives rise to the notion that one must be *guided*. If a rule, like a signpost, *could* be responded to in more than one way, then the explanation of our responding to it in the *same* way must be that the rule guides us in the right direction. But are we guided? If I am blindfolded and have to walk a narrow path, I will get into trouble unless someone takes my arm and draws me along the path. This is a genuine case of being guided. Nothing like that happens when I see a signpost on the road, or a sign on an escalator that says 'Keep to the right'. In actual cases I don't *feel* that I am being guided. 'Then there must be a guidance that you don't feel – an unconscious guidance.' This resort to an *intangible* guidance is only a desperate attempt to account for our agreement in responding to words and signs.

Another temptation is to think that if a person *understands* the meaning of the rule, then he will go on in the right way. This is true, but tautological. What criterion would there be for his having 'understood' the rule, other than his going on in the right way? A major theme of Wittgenstein's intensive thinking about the concept of 'following a rule', is that what is *primary* to following a rule lies not in interpretations, or in a mental state of understanding, but in actually *doing* in particular cases what *we* (the mature speakers of the language) call 'following the rule' (*PI*, 201).

People generally agree, not only in what is required by a rule, but also in their use of words to designate particular objects – words such as 'chair', 'house', 'tree'. We don't often get into quarrels as to whether some object is or isn't to be called a 'chair'. This is surprising since the things we call 'chairs' differ so greatly in shape, size, materials, structure, use. Certainly children learn this word without being introduced to a huge number of different sorts of chairs. Then why don't they seriously diverge in their use of the word?

It used to be said, and perhaps still is, that we 'abstract' the 'concept' of *chair* from the few examples of chairs with which we are presented: this is why we agree in our later applications of the word. This answer begs the question – for it assumes that all of us abstract the *same* concept. Furthermore, the notion of 'abstracting a concept' is deeply obscure. This phrase provides nothing more than a picture of something being drawn from something else – as a tooth is extracted from a jaw. There is embodied in this picture the assumption that a 'concept' is a unitary thing. But if we understand by a 'concept' the use of a word, then the idea of a concept as a definite unitary object vanishes. For example, we saw in Chapter 3 that the use of the word 'belief' fragments into a number of different uses. The same is true of the use of the word 'chair' or of any other common noun. The notion that the indefinite variety in the use of an expression could be 'abstracted' from examples becomes incomprehensible. We are left with the fact from which we started – that when people are given an initial instruction in the use of a word, an instruction that relies on only a few examples, they do go on to apply the word in new cases, largely agreeing with one another.

This common agreement in the application of words, and in what actions are required in order to follow a particular rule, is sometimes called by Wittgenstein 'agreement in *judgments*'.

> Understanding in language requires not only agreement in definitions, but also (queer as this may sound) agreement in judgments. This seems to abolish logic, but does not do so. – It is one thing to describe methods of measurement, and another to obtain and state results of measurement. But what we call 'measuring', is also determined by a certain constancy in the results of measurement.
>
> (*PI*, 242)

This means that when people measure, weigh, count, calculate, they generally obtain the same results. This constancy in results is necessary for the existence of these techniques. In judgments of colour there is widespread agreement: if there were not, our concept of colour would not exist (*Z*, 351). Mathematicians generally agree on the result of a calculation: if they did not we would not have our concept of 'mathematical certainty' (*PI*, p. 225). The practice of using people's names in addressing or calling them would not exist if people did not generally *remember* their own names (*OC*, 628).

AGREEMENT IN PRIMITIVE REACTIONS

Agreement exists in something more primitive than *judgments*. It extends to what is not 'intellectual' or 'rational' – to the natural expressions in behaviour of pain, fear, joy. In philosophy one is tempted to think that the physical behaviour of human beings is irrelevant to the *meaning* of the words 'pain' or 'fear' or 'joy'. It is assumed that each one of us learns 'from his own case' what these mental states are, without paying attention to his own or anyone else's behaviour. One purpose of Wittgenstein's so-called 'private language argument' is to show that if there were no characteristic expressions in behaviour of sensations and feeling, then our *concepts* of sensation and feeling would not exist.

Another notable phenomenon is a 'primitive' response to the

pain of *other* persons, not merely to one's own – a response of concern, sympathy, helping (*Z*, 540). By calling it 'primitive', Wittgenstein means that this reaction comes *before* linguistic learning, and is not the result of thought (*Z*, 541). The familiar philosophical explanation that 'we look after someone else because, by analogy with our own case, we believe that he too is experiencing pain' (*Z*, 542), is easily destroyed by criticism.

> Being sure that the other is in pain, doubting whether he is, and so on, are so many natural, instinctive, kinds of behaviour towards other human beings, and our language is merely an auxiliary to, and further extension of this behaviour. Our language game is an extension of primitive behaviour.
>
> (*Z*, 545)

The uses of language in which we speak of sensations and feelings, both of one's own and of others, did not emerge from reasoning. Instead they grow out of the unlearned behavioural expression of sensation and feeling, together with our common, instinctive, response to the plight of others.

PARTICULAR THOUGHTS

Will there be an explanation of why I had that particular thought just at that moment? Sometimes, yes; sometimes no. But this is unsatisfactory: it seems that there should be an explanation in every case.

Wittgenstein gives some illustrations of this assumption. He notes that there is such a thing as an impression or feeling of familiarity. In a crowded meeting, for example, I see a face that seems familiar to me. I think: 'I believe I have seen that man before.' This thought arose from an impression of familiarity. Wittgenstein also notes that there are feelings of 'old acquaintance', which are expressed in one's way of looking at something, or by the words 'The old room: just as it was!' (*PI*, 596). Also there are feelings of strangeness. I enter a room in which I have been many times previously; but now it feels strange to me. I think 'The furniture must have been changed.' This thought arose from that feeling of strangeness. So far, no philosophical assumption has entered the scene.

Such an assumption, however, does come in if I am inclined to think that *always* when I perceive something familiar I have a feeling of familiarity and always when I perceive something unfamiliar I have a feeling of strangeness. In fact this is not true – but the assumption is nourished by a certain image. Wittgenstein says:

> Because this feeling of strangeness does exist one cannot say that every object which we know well and does not seem strange to us, gives us a feeling of familiarity. – We think, as it were, that the place once filled by the feeling of strangeness must surely be occupied *somehow*. The place for this kind of atmosphere is there, and if one of them is not in possession of it, then another is.
>
> (*PI*, 596)

From the fact that sometimes when an object is familiar to us we have a feeling of familiarity, we are inclined to jump to the conclusion that *whenever* we perceive something familiar, we experience a feeling of familiarity. So if we have occasion to say, 'I am familiar with this neighbourhood', it seems that the neighbourhood *must feel* familiar. It is as if we said to ourselves: 'How could I *think* that an object is familiar, if I did not have a feeling of familiarity?' We postulate a feeling to explain a thought. As Wittgenstein puts it: 'When we do philosophy, we should like to hypostatize feelings, where there are none. They serve to explain our thoughts to us' (*PI*, 598). Often we can explain why a particular thought occurred to us. We are aware of its connections with a previous perception or thought or feeling. But sometimes we say, 'I don't know why that thought occurred to me just now.' *Must* there be an explanation? Wittgenstein is striving to eliminate these 'musts' from philosophical thinking. He says: 'In philosophy we do not draw conclusions. "But it must be like this!" is not a philosophical proposition. Philosophy only states what everyone admits' (*PI*, 599). In this remark Wittgenstein is not describing an actual procedure in philosophy. Instead, he is indicating what that procedure would be, if philosophy understood itself.

MEMORY

A conspicuous feature of philosophical thinking about memory has been the insistence that in remembering there must be an image, or copy, or picture, or mental representation, of what is remembered. Russell maintained that memory demands an image.

In fact, images are sometimes present, and sometimes not, when we remember or recall situations, events or objects that we have perceived, witnessed or experienced in the past. Why is there this demand that there must be an image, or 'something like an image', in remembering? Is it because of the idea that our recollections of past occurrences would not be based on *evidence* for our memory judgments:

> Memory: 'I see us still, sitting at that table.' – But do I really have the same visual image, or one of those I had then? Do I certainly see the table and my friend from the same point of view as then, and so not see myself? – My memory image is not evidence for that past situation, like a photograph which was taken then and convinces me now that this was how things were then. The memory image and the memory words stand on the *same* level.
>
> (*Z*, 650)

They stand on the same level! Neither has evidential priority over the other. My thoughts, my descriptions in words or drawings, my images, are *equally* expressions of what I recall. In the *Investigations* Wittgenstein makes a similar remark: 'The words with which I express my memory are my memory-reaction' (*PI*, 343). The words do not require the support of images.

Psychology swarms with theories of recognition – the recognizing of faces, figures, patterns. One type of theory is called 'template-matching'. The idea is that when a particular pattern is first perceived, a prototype or template of it is deposited in the mind (or in the central nervous system), and incoming patterns are tested against it. If there is a match, recognition has taken place. This theory employs the notion of a comparison between two impressions. It has a naive appeal. Here is Wittgenstein's comment:

> It is easy to have a false picture of the occurrences called 'recognizing'; as if recognizing always consisted in comparing two impressions with one another. It is as if I carried a picture of an object with me and identified an object as the one represented by the picture. Our memory seems to us to mediate such a comparison, by preserving a picture of what was seen before, or by allowing us to look into the past (as through a telescope).
>
> (*PI*, 604)

Sometimes we recognize a person by means of a photograph, or a difficult-to-remember colour by means of a colour sample. The template theory is motivated by the false notion that *all* recognition is mediated by a comparison.

Recent psychology and philosophy have moved strongly towards 'physicalism' or 'materialism' (away from 'mentalism'). Theories of memory and recognition no longer invoke mental images, but instead physical 'traces' in the brain. The basic assumption is still at work: some sort of 'comparison' must take place between a present perception and a 'residue' of the past, such as a neural trace. The dominant feeling is that memory and recognition *without* physiological memory traces, would be 'magical'. (In a machine it *would* be magical.)

Wittgenstein does not defend magic; but he does challenge the assumption that recognition and remembering *require* that traces of previous experience be stored in the nervous system:

> I saw this man years ago: now I have seen him again, I recognize him, I remember his name. And why does there have to be a cause of this remembering in my nervous system? Why must something, whatever it may be, be stored there *in any form*? Why *must* a trace have been left behind? Why shouldn't there be a psychological regularity to which *no* physiological regularity corresponds? If this overthrows our conceptions of causality, then it is time they were overthrown.
>
> (*Z*, 610)

If a person describes a past event from memory, this presupposes that he previously witnessed, or previously learned of the event – otherwise it would not be called 'remembering'. But it does *not* presuppose that a record of the past event was stored in his nervous system. The assumption of traces is alien to the meaning of the words 'remembering' and 'recognizing'. Remembering and recognizing are commonplace phenomena – there is nothing 'magical' about them. In our actual practice with these words, the assumption of physiological traces has no role whatever. It is a foreign import into the concept of memory – a gratuitous demand of 'theory'.

Memory and recognition are normal human powers. Creatures that did not have them would not be human. We can predict, with considerable success, that a person who witnessed a startling event a week ago, will now be able to describe, more or less accurately, what took place. This prediction is based on the *history* of the person: 'He was there and saw it; so he will be able to tell us what happened.' Witnessing an event and later recalling it: this is a psychological regularity in human life. Philosophical and psychological theories of memory arise because the theorists cannot accept this regularity as a plain fact. They try to *explain* it by introducing an intermediary – a retained mental image, or a physiological trace – to bridge the temporal gap between the witnessing and subsequent recollection. When we scrutinize these intermediaries, we realize that they are powerless to do the trick. We should realize that the psychological regularity of 'witnessing–recalling' is a basic form of life, a feature of the natural history of human beings – something to be accepted as it is, not to be explained. As Wittgenstein says: 'What has to be accepted, the given, is – one could say – *forms of life*' (*PI*, p. 226). And in a private notebook he wrote: 'May God grant to the philosopher insight into what lies before everyone's eyes' (*VB*, p. 163).

KNOWING WHAT ONE WAS ABOUT TO SAY

This is a phenomenon to which Wittgenstein pays extraordinary attention, and which other philosophers have scarcely noticed. In conversation you were about to make a remark but were interrupted. Later someone asks, 'What were you going to say?' Your reply might be, 'I don't remember.' Or, after a struggle to recall, you might exclaim, 'Now I know what I was going to say' – and then proceed to say it.

What is puzzling about this familiar phenomenon? There is an inclination to think that if now you know what you were going to say, then you must have said or thought it to yourself, *before* you were about to speak, but that would be unusual. Only rarely does one, in quick conversation, say or think something to oneself before saying it aloud.

Another attempt at explanation is to say that you must have read off, or inferred, what you were going to say, from the remembered details of the past situation. Relevant details could be of the following sort: that another person had said such-and-such, and that someone else objected 'No! No!', that there was laughter, that you felt irritated. So you gathered from these remembered details, what you were about to say.

Wittgenstein points out, with marvellous acuteness, that more than one interpretation of those details would be possible; and further, that you did not *choose* between interpretations (*PI*, 634). He remarks further:

'I was going to say. . . .' – You remember various details. But not even all of them together show this intention. It is as if a snapshot of a scene had been taken, but only a few scattered details of it were to be seen: here a hand, there a bit of a face, or a hat – the rest is dark. And now it is as if I knew quite certainly what the whole picture represents. As if I could read the darkness.

(PI, 635)

This is a striking comparison with a snapshot that presents only a few details of a scene. The point of the final sentence is that if I did derive my account of what I was about to say from those details, then it would be like 'reading the darkness'.

So how are we to explain this phenomenon of my knowing what I was going to say? It is right, of course, to say that I remembered what I was going to say. But this does not solve the problem. For this is a surprising use of the word 'remember'. To see this we need only ask: how could I remember what I was about to say, since I did not say it to myself beforehand? Wittgenstein continues:

'I know exactly what I was going to say!' And yet I did not say it. – And I don't read it off from some other occurrence which took place then and which I remember. And I don't interpret that situation and its antecedents. For I don't consider them and don't judge them.

(PI, 637)

This phenomenon of knowing what one was going to say has an interesting bearing on the perennial attempts in philosophy to define the concept of knowledge. Knowing what one was going to say certainly is a form of knowledge. It presents a natural use of the word 'know'.

What might be called the 'canonical' philosophical analysis of 'I know that p', holds that this statement is true if and only if the following three conditions are satisfied:

1 I believe that p;
2 p is true;
3 my belief that p is based on adequate evidence.

I will not consider here conditions (1) and (2), but only condition (3). This requirement is not satisfied by the familiar phenomenon of 'knowing what one was going to say'. This use of 'know' is not

69

based on any evidence – and so not on evidence that is adequate, satisfactory or convincing. *Evidence* does not pertain to this employment of 'know'. We do not ask a person what his evidence is for his declaration that he knows what he was going to say. This is not a matter of politeness. No sort of evidence, either 'inner' or 'outer', enters the scene.

At first sight this seems to be an extraordinary use of language. But actually it is common and ordinary. It only looks strange when we approach it from a certain direction. Our scientific and technological culture has accustomed us to expect explanations. When we realize that normally there is no explanation of how one knows what one was going to say, this phenomenon strikes us as remarkable.

There is a closely related phenomenon from which the same point emerges. Sometimes we make admissions of this sort: 'For a moment I intended to deceive him.' Here again there is an inclination to ask, 'How do you know that for a moment you intended to deceive him? Aren't you interpreting the few details which you remember, and wouldn't a different interpretation be possible?'

We have noted Wittgenstein's observation that the declaration 'I was going to say...', is not 'read off' from anything that occurred at that time; nor is it due to an interpretation of the situation. Wittgenstein considers this new example, confessing that he too has an inclination to view the statement, 'For a moment I intended to deceive him', as an interpretation.

> How does it come about that nevertheless I am inclined to see an interpretation in saying 'For a moment I was going to deceive him'?
> 'How can you be certain that for the space of a moment you were going to deceive him? Weren't your actions and your thoughts much too rudimentary?'
> For can't the evidence be too scanty? Yes, when one looks into it, it seems extraordinarily scanty; but isn't this because one is taking no account of the history of this evidence? Certain antecedents were necessary for me to have had a momentary intention of pretending to someone else that I was unwell. If someone says 'For a moment ...' is he really only describing a momentary occurrence?
> But not even the whole story was my evidence for saying 'For a moment ...'.
>
> (*PI*, 638)

Suppose my momentary intention was to pretend that I was ill. When Wittgenstein says that certain antecedents were necessary for that intention to exist, he does not mean 'causally' necessary, but 'logically' necessary. 'Pretending to be ill' makes sense only in special circumstances. For example, I am employed and am expected to turn up for work: but I have a strong reason for being somewhere else – then 'pretending to be ill' would have sense.

But the most important point in Wittgenstein's remarks is that neither the whole history of the situation, nor any details of what went through my mind, would be my evidence for saying, 'For a moment I had the intention to lie.' Certain circumstances were necessary for my statement to make sense. But they did not constitute my evidence for the statement. My statement was not based on evidence: but that does not mean that evidence was *lacking*. It means that 'evidence' plays no part in this use of language, in this description of past intention. Any more than it does in the description of *present* intention.

Wittgenstein presents the point with striking clarity in *Zettel*:

If I say 'I was then going to do such-and-such', and if this statement is based on the thoughts, images, etc., then someone else to whom I tell only these thoughts, images, etc., ought to be able to infer with as great a certainty as mine, that I was then going to do such-and-such. – But often he could not do it. Indeed, were I myself to infer my intention from the evidence, other people would be right to say that this conclusion was very uncertain.

(*Z*, 41)

There will, of course, be an inclination to say: 'But the intention itself was an event, an inner occurrence. So why could not my memory of *it* be my evidence for my statement?'

This inclination comes from a false picture of intention. Wittgenstein comments on that picture: 'Intention is neither an emotion, a mood, nor yet a sensation or image. It is not a state of consciousness. It does not have genuine duration' (*Z*, 45). An intention is not something 'going on', in the sense of the flowing of water through a pipe. It is not something I could observe, and take note of its starting or stopping, its increasing or decreasing – as I can do with a sensation. It is not an experience, like a sudden fright or a burst of panic. Wittgenstein comments on the notion that an intention is an 'inner experience':

71

'For a moment I meant to ...'. That is, I had a particular feeling, an inner experience; and I remember it. – And now remember *quite precisely*! Then the 'inner experience' of intending seems to vanish. Instead one remembers thoughts, feelings, movements, and also connections with earlier situations.

(PI, 645)

If I try to remember what occurred in my mind during that moment when I intended to deceive the person in front of me, I might remember my thought 'Will he believe me?', my image of his face becoming angry, my fear that I would be found out. But the intention itself would not be an item in that remembered passage of my mental experience. To paraphrase a remark of Wittgenstein: 'If God had looked into my mind he would not have been able to see my intention' (see *PI*, p. 217). God could have seen my image, my fear, my thought, but not my intention – for an intention is not a state of consciousness, not an event in one's content of immediate experience.

SUMMARY

We have noted a variety of failed explanations of characteristic phenomena of our lives. Some of these explanations are the following: that the mastering of a language is due to the innate possession of the grammar of all possible languages; that the lower animals don't employ language because they lack the mental capacity; that people think because thinking has been found to be advantageous; that a person is able to follow a rule because he interprets the rule correctly, or because the rule guides him to the right action; that speakers of a language largely agree in their employment of words because they have abstracted and internalized the appropriate concepts; that you come to the aid of an injured person because, by analogy with your own case, you believe that he suffers pain; that we judge an object to be familiar to us because it produces in us a feeling of familiarity; that memory judgments of past events depend on images or other mental representations of those events; that the recognition of faces or patterns is due to their being matched with stored 'templates' derived from previous perception; that memory and recognition would be 'magical' without the existence of physiological memory traces; that a person knows what he was going to say, either because he had already said it to himself or because he inferred it from the details of the remembered situation; that if someone had a momentary intention to do such-and-such, his later knowledge that he had that intention was either due to his having inferred it from the situation, or due to his having observed the intention as an item in his conscious experience.

Wittgenstein's criticism of these explanations sometimes takes the form of showing them to be falsely generalized: sometimes tautological; sometimes simply nonsensical; sometimes gratuitous. When we perceive the futility of trying to explain these phenomena, then we can focus on the phenomena themselves, and even be awakened to a kind of *wonder* at their existence. In an unpublished manuscript, written in 1941, Wittgenstein wrote: 'People who always keep asking "Why?" resemble tourists who read Baedeker while they stand before a building and through reading about the building's history, origins, and so on are kept from *seeing* it' (*VB*, 40).

NOTE

1 Quoted by G. Hallett, *A Companion to Wittgenstein's 'Philosophical Investigations'*, Ithaca and London, Cornell University Press, 1977, pp. 496–7.

6

THE LIMIT OF
EXPLANATION

Philosophy simply puts everything before us, and neither explains nor deduces anything.

(*PI*, 126)

Wittgenstein is here proposing a radical change in our conception of
what philosophy should be doing. To say that philosophy does not
seek to explain anything is certainly not a true description of philosophy as it has been, and still is, practised. Many philosophers would
be dumbfounded or outraged by the suggestion that they should not
be seeking explanations. The traditional aim of philosophy has been
to explain the essential nature of justice, right and wrong, duty, the
good, beauty, art, language, rules, thought. A philosopher may well
ask: 'What am I supposed to do if not to explain?'

In Wittgenstein's later thinking there is an answer. The task of
philosophy is to *describe*. Describe *what?* Describe *concepts*. How does
one describe a concept? By describing the use of the word, or of
those words, that express the concept. This is what philosophy
should 'put before us'.

The description of the use of a word is called by Wittgenstein
describing the 'language-game' with that word. But he did not think
that one is called upon to describe the use of a word in its *totality*.
Only those features of the use of a word which give rise to philosophical perplexity need to be described. This 'putting before us' the
use of a word includes *comparing* and *contrasting* its use with the use of
other words. The words 'reason' and 'cause', for example, have a
use that is similar in some respects, and different in other respects.

The noting of these differences may take us by surprise – even though they are familiar words of daily language.

Describing the use of an expression is also called by Wittgenstein 'describing the *grammar*' of the expression. Describing language-games and describing grammar come to the same.

But it would be a serious misunderstanding if one thought that describing language-games, or describing grammar, only amounted to giving an account of sentence-construction or syntax. Early in the *Investigations* Wittgenstein says: 'Here the term "language *game*" is meant to bring into prominence the fact that the *speaking* of language is part of an activity, or a form of life' (*PI*, 23). This means that in describing the language-game, or some part of the language-game with a word, one is describing how that word is embedded in actions and reactions – in human behaviour. If, for example, a man firmly announces that he intends to quit his job, his wife and friends may try to dissuade him, his employer may start looking for a replacement, his wife may cancel an order for new furniture. The simple words 'I intend to quit my job', may generate many reactions, and even bitter acrimony. The possible consequences of this announcement will depend on various circumstances – on whether other persons depend on this man for support, whether other employment is readily available and so on.

On the other hand, the announcement may not produce even a ripple of reaction if, for example, it is well known that this man frequently does not carry out his announced intentions. This point displays an important feature of the grammar of the word 'intention'. When a person declares his intention to do so-and-so, this normally creates the presumption that he will *do* it. Other persons have the right to *expect* him to do it, and to make their own plans accordingly. If he doesn't do it, they have a right to demand an explanation. This is not a *moral* but a *logical* right. It belongs to the grammar of the words 'I intend to do X', that others are entitled to expect the speaker to do X. If a person never, or hardly ever, carried out his announced intention, then his words would no longer be taken seriously. His 'I intend' might be treated the same as 'I would like'. An implicit promise of *doing* is part of the meaning of 'I intend'.

The fact that the announcement 'I intend to ...' has its place in a network of action and reaction is an illustration of Wittgenstein's remark that speaking a language is part of a 'form of life'. It is also an illustration of these striking remarks: 'Words have meaning only in the flow of thought and life' (*Z*, 173). 'Our talk gets its sense from the rest of our actions' (*OC*, 229). The word 'intention' is embedded in a particular pattern of human activity. The person who declares his intention normally *acts* on it: he carries it out. Or if he does not, he is normally ready to provide an explanation – something unforeseen prevented him, or he had a reason for changing his mind. These are explanations *within* the language-game with the word 'intention'.

So the language-game provides a place for explanations, for reasons and justifications. For reasons for having that intention; for explanation and justification for not fulfilling it. But there is no explanation for the existence of this language-game. There is no explanation for that particular form of life, that pattern of action and reaction, with which the word 'intention' is internally connected. It was not invented by people because they foresaw some advantage in it, as they invent tools and machines. It was not invented at all – any more than was talking or thinking. The use of the word 'intention' and the pattern of activity with which it is bound up is transmitted from generation to generation. It is one of our forms of life – part of our culture. There could be a people who did not have any word that functions like our word 'intention', nor engaged in that related pattern of activity – just as there could be a people who did not have our interest in sport, or in art.

Another noteworthy language-game is the one with the word 'motive'. If a person does something unusual we may wonder what his motive was, and may indulge in various conjectures. Normally, however, the quickest and surest way of finding out is to ask *him*. Now of course he may not reveal it: perhaps he himself does not understand it, or perhaps he misrepresents it both to himself and to others. But what is highly interesting is that if he does disclose his motive, typically his acknowledgement of it will not be based on any *inference* from the situation, or from his own behaviour or previous actions – as would be the conjecture of others. He *tells* us his motive, *without* inference.

This can appear to us as a surprising use of language. Wittgenstein says: 'Let yourself be *struck* by the existence of such a thing as our language game: confessing the motive of my action' (*PI*, p. 224). We cannot explain why this use of language exists. All we can do is to describe it – and *behold* it! In *On Certainty* there is a general comment about language-games: 'You must bear in mind that the language game is, so to speak, something unforeseeable. I mean: it is not based on grounds. Not reasonable (or unreasonable). It stands there – like our life' (*OC*, 559). This is a deeply significant observation. For one thing, it provides a sharp contrast with the *Tractatus* – which says: 'The existence of a general form of propositions is proved by the fact that there cannot be a proposition whose form could not have been foreseen (i.e., constructed)' (*T*, 4.5). In Chapter 3 we noted how Wittgenstein's new thinking broke away from his previous conviction that there was a general form of propositions, an essential nature of propositions, an essence of language. This means that there is no common nature of *saying something* – that the phenomena of language have no formal unity. According to the new conception a sentence has meaning only within a particular language-game. The language-games are internally connected with human activities, forms of life. And think how the latter have changed in the last thousand years! Think how different is the life of a present-day city dweller, in activities and preoccupations, from that of nomads and peasants of a previous age. These changes in modes of living create unforeseeable uses of language. Just as the development of the last two centuries in music and painting (which are ways of 'saying' something) could not have been anticipated by the ancient Egyptians.

A second point to be noted in the remark from *On Certainty* is the comparison between our language-games and our human life. Both are unforeseeable and inexplicable. But this is not actually a comparison of two separate things. For what would this life of ours be without the language-games? Every preoccupation, every striving, every emotion – seeks its expression in language. But this expression is not an exterior adornment. Certainly there could be no criticism or reflection without language. Nor anything that would come close to resembling human love, or hope, or hatred or joy. The observation and description of language-games, if it is sensitive and detailed, is actually a study of human life.

Wittgenstein regarded the language-games, and their associated forms of life, as beyond explanation. The inescapable logic of this conception is that the terms 'explanation', 'reason', 'justification', have a use *exclusively within* the various language-games. The word 'explanation' appears in many language-games, and is used differently in different games. My explanation of *my* motive, for example, is a different concept of 'explanation' from my explanation of *your* motive. An explanation of why your car won't start will be radically different in kind from an explanation of why a friend of yours is avoiding you.

An explanation is *internal* to a particular language-game. There is no explanation that *rises above* our language-games, and explains *them*. This would be a *super-concept* of explanation – which means that it is an ill-conceived fantasy.

In the *Tractatus* Wittgenstein thought that the occurrence of any particular event is not explicable. The world consists ultimately of elementary facts, which are independent of one another. It is an illusion to suppose that the Laws of Nature explain *why* things occur as they do. But *concepts*, he assumed, can be explained (including the concept of *language*) in the special sense of being *definable* in terms of the necessary and sufficient conditions of their application.

In the *Investigations* the assumption that our ordinary concepts are capable of strict definition is rejected. Explanation-by-definition is discarded as a primary technique of philosophy. There continues to be agreement with the *Tractatus* that the Laws of Nature do not *compel* anything to happen. As regards 'explanation', the new view is that there are many different concepts of 'explanation', each one operating in a particular language-game. But a language-game itself rests on no grounds that explain or justify *it*, that show it to be reasonable or unreasonable. It can only be observed and described.

If philosophy cannot explain why anything happens or exists; if it cannot reveal the essential nature of anything – then what function remains for it? In the new conception the subject matter of philosophy just is *philosophical confusion*. Who is prone to this confusion? Not merely those who are professionally engaged with philosophy, as university teachers or writers. *All of us* tend to become entangled in our concepts, even when the topics of discussion and controversy are not explicitly philosophical. Expressions such as 'human character', 'historical explanation', 'psychological causation', 'freedom', readily contribute to misunderstanding and bafflement.

The task of philosophy is not to explain deep mysteries, but to bring clarification and therefore *light* to our thinking. By careful description of the use of a word, it will show how this same word changes in meaning from one context to another. This descriptive work of philosophy is not theoretical. It is not a search for exact definitions of perplexing concepts, since they do not *have* exact definitions. It will not formulate hypotheses to explain why we have *these* concepts instead of other ones. Wittgenstein says:

And we may not advance any kind of theory. There must not be anything hypothetical in our considerations. We must do away with all *explanation*, and description alone must take its place. And this description gets its light, that is to say, its purpose, from the philosophical problems.

(PI, 109)

What are called philosophical 'problems' are actually confusions – confusions about our own concepts, the grammar of our own language, our familiar language-games. A striking feature of philosophical misunderstanding is that it pertains to something that we already *know*. We know how to use words such as 'believe', 'know', 'expect', 'remember' – we use them confidently and correctly every day. This is why Wittgenstein says: 'Since everything lies open to view there is nothing to explain' *(PI, 126)*. That which confuses us, but at the same time 'lies open to view', is the grammar of our own language. A philosopher cannot teach this to us – we learned it a long time ago. What he can do is to *remind* us of something we already know. He can remind us of fine differences between concepts – differences which we observe *in practice* in our everyday activities – but which we tend to forget when we engage in intellectual reflection.

In the past philosophers have frequently supposed that their mission was to reveal the general features of reality, or the hidden mechanisms of thinking and perception – and so on. But as early as 1931 Wittgenstein had arrived at the realization that there is *nothing* to be discovered! In a conversation he said:

The wrong conception to which I want to object in this connection is the following, that we can come on something which today we cannot yet see, that we can discover something wholly new. That is a mistake. The truth of the matter is that we have already got everything, and we have got it actually *present*; we need not wait for anything. We make our moves in the realm of the grammar of our ordinary language, and this grammar is already there. Thus we have already got everything and need not wait for the future.[1]

Everything necessary for the clarification and solution of philosophical problems is already in our possession. These 'problems' are simply our own misconceptions about the grammar of our own language. We move about in this grammar every day. In order to remove our misconceptions, no theorizing is called for. What is required is only that we *look* at the grammar which is at our command. As Wittgenstein says: 'Don't think, but look!' (*PI*, 66).

One might imagine that philosophers would react with relief and joy to Wittgenstein's view that everything necessary for the treatment of philosophical problems 'lies before us', that 'nothing is hidden'. But, in fact, this is not so. Wittgenstein's writings have not had a *great* impact on present-day philosophical work. Many individuals have been influenced – but the major tendency continues to be to formulate theories: theories about the nature of *meaning*, of *thinking*, of *representation*, of *belief* and so on.

Why is this? It is difficult to understand. Perhaps the weight of philosophy's past, the tradition of theorizing, is too great. Perhaps the temptation to think that behind the multiple uses of words like 'cause' or 'remember', there is hidden the 'real nature' of causation or of memory, is overwhelming. Perhaps there is a desire to share in the prestige of science, which does discover new objects and processes in nature.

But for one who is able to resist these pressures, Wittgenstein's conception of philosophy can be truly bracing. To engage in the kind of grammatical investigation that Wittgenstein endorses, one must first of all admit to being confused about some concept. By way of illustration let us return to the concept of 'intention', and let us take as an example a philosopher who cannot help thinking that a person's intention is some sort of inner occurrence, which *causes* the intended action. The philosopher also becomes aware that his preferred notion of 'causation' is that of a relation between 'logically distinct' events. But as he studies the grammar of 'intention' he realizes that *this* notion of a 'causal relation' cannot hold between an intention and the intended action. For in the ordinary, everyday employment of the word 'intention', the description of one's intention is nothing other than the description of one's intended action. Therefore intention and intended action are not 'logically distinct' events, in the sense required by his preferred notion of 'causation'. This philosopher will have corrected an error in his thinking, and so will have advanced his understanding of the concept of intention – although, no doubt, other snares await him.

It would be useless for some other philosopher to protest against the ordinary use of the word 'intention' – to insist that there *must* be a description of an intention, other than the description of what is intended. For philosophy cannot teach us how to speak; it cannot reform our language. As Wittgenstein remarks:

80

> Philosophy may in no way interfere with the actual use of
> language; in the end it can only describe it.
> Nor can it give it any foundation. It leaves everything as it is.
>
> (*PI*, 124)

Philosophy leaves everything *in language* as it is – this employment of
words, this grammar. Philosophy can only seek to unravel the confusions that beset us because we are misled by surface similarities
between our linguistic expressions. We say: 'He remembers his former anguish'; and also 'He remembered his previous intention'. This
may make it look as if 'anguish' and 'intention' are *both* concepts of
states of immediate consciousness. But they are not. Why not?
There can be no explanation.

> Our mistake is to look for an explanation where we should see
> the facts as 'primary phenomena' [*Urphänomene*]. That is, where
> we should say: *this language game is played.*
>
> (*PI*, 654)

> The question is not one of explaining a language game by our
> experiences, but of observing a language game.
>
> (*PI*, 655)

Our actual employment of words, our language-games, *as they are* –
this is the ground to which philosophy must turn in its attempt to
display conceptual differences. This is *the given* for philosophy. This
is where explanation comes to an end.

The realization that the language-games can be described, but
not explained may create the feeling that there is something *mysterious* about them. But they are not mysterious in the sense of being
dark or inscrutable or unfamiliar. The feeling of mystery arises
because of our unreasonable demand that *everything* should be explained.

The fact that the language-games are beyond explanation is not a
small fact but a great one. In speaking of 'language-games', we are
speaking of our lives. A 'language-game' is an employment of language that is embedded in one of the innumerable patterns of
human life. Certainly we can easily feel that human life is mysterious. All of us, on certain occasions, are struck by the mystery of
birth and death – of the search for love – of hope, despair, terror,
hatred, grief – of trust and joy. We feel the mystery of a loving heart
– of genuineness, simplicity, courage, truthfulness. These are things
we marvel at.

Our language-games, our concepts – of jealousy, resentment, fear, love, forgiveness and so on – span all of human life. We speak of these things in words – words that are bound up with the human actions, gestures, reactions, emotions, thoughts – with all of the expressions of human life, from which the words draw their meaning.

Within many concepts there is a space for *reasons*. One may say: 'Why do I trust that man? Because in the past he has served me well.' So here a reason is given for trust. But if we say of a small child, 'She clung to her father trustingly', we do not expect the child to give a reason for trusting her father: and indeed there is no sense in supposing that *she* has a reason. So sometimes a person has a reason for trust, and sometimes not. Why is one and the same word used in these different ways? There is no explanation. This is just the way it is.

Consider the phenomenon of 'telling a dream'. How strange that there should be such a thing. It is possible that there should be a whole community of people in which this phenomenon did not occur. These people would not have the concept of a dream – or, at least, not exactly *our* concept.

There could be a society in which no one gave orders to anyone. There could be a community in which the writing and reading of poetry did not occur; nor composing and listening to music; nor telling jokes. One could not explain why those people do *not* have those forms of life – nor why we *do* have them. Neither philosophy nor science can explain this. What philosophy can do is to correct our inclination to assume, because of superficial similarities, that different language-games and forms of life are really the same. (For example, that when you tell a dream that is 'just like' reporting a scene you witnessed on the street.)

Wittgenstein's emphasized theme – that reasons, justifications, explanations come to an end – does not mean that there are no reasons, justifications, explanations, for anything. For these concepts do have a place within the boundaries of many of our language-games. Nor does it mean that we do not have the time or energy to go on giving reasons and explanations. What it means is that these come to an end *somewhere*. Where is that? It is at *the existence* of the language-games and the associated forms of life. There is where explanation has reached its limit. There reasons stop. In philosophy we can only notice the language-games, describe them, and sometimes wonder at them.

NOTE

1 Brian McGuinness (ed.), *Wittgenstein and the Vienna Circle*, conversations recorded by Friedrich Waismann, tr. Joachim Schulte and Brian McGuinness, Oxford, Blackwell, 1979, p. 138.

7

FOUR ANALOGIES

In the Introduction I indicated that there is a link between Wittgenstein's philosophical outlook and a religious view of the world. This link is perhaps better called 'analogy' than 'resemblance'. The first analogy pertains to the concept of *explanation*: how it reaches a limit, and when pressed further loses its sense.

For many people the conception of God has no serious significance: religious belief is regarded as something ridiculous, an infantile superstition. There are others who take a serious view of religion, but regard it as a harmful influence, an obstacle to the fullest and best development of humanity.

Yet there are many people, even in this technological and materialistic age, who observe religious practices – praying to God for help, asking Him for forgiveness, thanking Him for the blessings of this life – and who thereby gain comfort and strength, hope and cheerfulness. Many of these people would have no understanding of what it would *mean* to provide a 'rational justification' for their religious belief – nor do they feel a need for it. Many would regard their faith as itself an undeserved *gift* from God. When overwhelmed by calamity, they arrive at a kind of reconciliation once they come to feel that these sufferings are God's will. They would see no sense in asking *why* God willed these troubles to occur. To speak of God's will is, for them, an end to explanation. When Wittgenstein said that all he wanted was that his philosophical work 'should be God's will', he would certainly have considered any question as to *why* it should be God's will as nonsensical.

The analogy to philosophy is that reasons, justifications, explana-

84

tions, reach a terminus in the language-games and their internally related forms of human life. The assumption that *everything* can be explained filled Wittgenstein with a kind of fury.

Consider the example of the language-game of *promising*. A person promises to do something. This creates in others the expectation that the promise will be fulfilled. If it is not, these others have a justification for reproaching that person, or for demanding an explanation for the non-fulfilment. Not just any answer will be *called* an 'explanation' – certainly not, 'I just didn't feel like it.'

We can think of the language-game of promising as a peculiar institution, a surprising practice. Within the institution there is a place for explanations – of why the promise was given; of why it was not fulfilled. But can the existence of this institution be explained? Could there not be human communities in which it did not exist? Do *we* have it because somebody thought it would be useful? Do we have any understanding of what it would be like to *explain* the existence of this particular pattern of action and reaction?

There could be a people who did no calculations or made no measurements. Their lives would be less sophisticated than ours. But that is no explanation of why *we* engage in those practices.

Philosophy can observe a complicated linguistic practice and describe how one movement in it is related to another. But philosophy cannot explain why the practice exists: nor can the 'hard' sciences of physics, chemistry, biology; nor the 'soft' sciences of psychology, sociology, anthropology.

A religious practice is itself a language-game – a pattern in which words and gestures are interwoven in acts of worship, prayer, confession, absolution, thanksgiving. Religious practices are a part of the natural history of mankind and are no more explicable than are other features of this natural history. It is not an *explanation* to say that religious practice arises from 'a basic religious impulse' – any more than it is to say that bodies fall toward the earth because of the force of gravity. The existence of religious practices can no more be explained than can the existence of sports, or of musical composition.

In religious thinking there is frequent reference to 'the will of God'. These words put an end to the demand for explanation: at the deepest religious level there is no asking for God's reason or justification. But is the reference to the will of God *itself* an explanation? It may look like one. But is that the actual functioning of the words 'the will of God', in religious life? I believe not. To say 'It is the will of God' is not to offer an *explanation* of why your child died, or why the hurricane destroyed your home, or why you and your friends were cruelly tortured. If it were meant as an explanation, then the *same* explanation would explain everything: why the wind blew, and why it did not; why the rivers overflowed, and why they ran dry; why you became ill, and why you were spared. An explanation that explains everything that occurs in the same way, actually explains nothing. The reference to God's will can, in a religious setting, give comfort: but not everything that gives comfort is an explanation.

The function of the words, 'It is God's will', when said religiously and seriously, in a time of trouble, is not to offer the *final* explanation, nor any explanation at all. Instead, they are an attempt to bring to an end the torment of asking '*Why* did it have to happen?' – an attempt to give the tormented one rest, to provide *peace*.

In secular life, when something distressing occurs and there is a demand for explanations of why it happened – at some stage someone may say: 'It is pointless to continue seeking for an explanation. We are faced with a fact which we must *accept*. That's how it is!' The words, 'It is God's will', have many religious connotations: but they also have a logical force similar to 'That's how it is!' Both expressions tell us to stop asking 'Why?' and instead to *accept a fact*!

The analogy with the language-games is clear. Wittgenstein says: 'It might be asked: how did human beings ever come to make the verbal utterances which we call reports of past wishes or past intentions?' (*PI*, 656). Since we have no idea of what an answer might be, it would be wiser to stop trying to satisfy this craving for an explanation. 'The question is not one of explaining a language game by means of our experiences, but of noting a language game' (*PI*, 655). 'Look on the language game as what is *primary*!' (*PI*, 656). You make a study of a particular language-game. Then you can say to someone: 'Look at it! That's how it is! Don't ask why, but take it as a fact, without explanation!' We need 'to *accept* the everyday language game' (*PI*, p. 200).

A second and closely related analogy between religious thinking and Wittgenstein's philosophical thought is the following: in his 'Lecture on ethics' of 1929, Wittgenstein said that sometimes he 'wondered at the existence of the world', and that he thought that this was the experience of 'seeing the world as a miracle'. Religious writers often speak of 'the miracle of God's world'.

In scientific, cosmological speculation there are theories about 'the origin' of the universe – e.g. 'the big bang'. But, in so far as I understand them, these are theories about 'the first state' of the universe, from which everything else is supposed to have developed. They are not theories as to *why anything exists at all*; and it does not seem that it could be the business of science to offer a theory about that.

In the *Investigations* and other late writings, Wittgenstein sometimes expressed a kind of wonder at the existence of the various language-games and their contained forms of human action and reaction. 'Let yourself be *struck* by the existence of such a thing as our language game of: confessing the motive of my action' (*PI*, p. 224). Old language-games go out of existence; new ones arise. But what will happen in language is unpredictable. New language-games are not based on grounds or reasons, and therefore cannot be foreseen. You cannot say, for example, that our use of the word 'hope' came into existence in order to express our feeling of hope – as if hope could be fully formed in the absence of language. 'Can only those hope who can talk? Only those who have mastered the use of a language. That is, the phenomena of hope are modes of this complicated form of life' (*PI*, p. 174). A language-game simply *is there*. You can observe it, describe it – but not explain *why* it is there.

The religious sense of seeing the world as a miracle has its analogue in a kind of astonishment at the inexplicable existence of the human language-games. This philosophical astonishment is not a religious sense of the miraculous – for it does not view the language-games as *sacred*. But in respect to the feeling of wonder and mystery, it is analogous to the religious sense of the miracle of the world and the miracle of human life.

A third analogy is the following: religious emotion, thinking, practice, are an expression of the conviction that something is *basically wrong* with human beings. We pursue the idols of wealth or status; we want to be admired; even our love is contaminated by jealousy, resentment, hatred; we are quickly offended and slow to forgive; scarcely ever do we love others as we love ourselves; we do little in the way of giving drink to those who thirst and food to those who hunger; we are beset by anxieties; we fear death. There is a kind of moral and spiritual illness that possesses us, even when we think we are healthy.

That is how a genuinely religious person thinks and feels about *himself*. As Wittgenstein puts it: 'People are religious in the degree that they believe themselves to be not so much *imperfect*, as *ill*' (*VB*, p. 45).

87

Now it is interesting that Wittgenstein employs the terms 'illness' and 'disease' (*Krankheit*), when he is trying to characterize the manoeuvres and expedients to which we resort in philosophical theorizing, when searching for explanations. In the *Brown Book* he says: 'There is a kind of general disease of thinking which always looks for (and finds) what would be called a mental state from which all our acts spring as from a reservoir' (*BB*, p. 145). Thus the actions of obeying an order or following a rule flow from the reservoir of one's state of understanding the order or the rule. A person's reports of what he witnessed proceed from the reservoir of his memory.

This same movement of philosophical thinking is sometimes described by Wittgenstein as the postulating of 'intermediary steps'.

> We are treating here of cases in which, as one might roughly put it, the grammar of a word seems to suggest the 'necessity' of a certain intermediary step, although in fact the word is used in cases in which there is no such intermediary step. Thus we are inclined to say: 'A person *must* understand an order before he obeys it', 'He must know where his pain is before he can point to it', 'He must know the tune before he can sing it', and suchlike.
>
> (*BB*, p. 130)

The craziness of much of philosophical theorizing comes from yielding to the temptation to explain everyday actions, reactions, abilities, by inventing 'reservoirs' of mental states, intermediary steps, underlying mechanisms.

Consider the following simple example. In a schoolroom the teacher has asked a question on the subject of study, and awaits a response.

> Think of putting your hand up in school. Need you have rehearsed the answer silently to yourself, in order to have the right to put your hand up? And *what* must have gone on inside you – Nothing. But it is important that you usually know an answer when you put your hand up; and that is the criterion of your *understanding* the act of putting your hand up.
>
> (*Z*, 136)

A pupil who never gave an answer, but insisted on putting up his hand, would show a failure to understand the *meaning* of this act of putting up one's hand. This does *not* imply, however, that something

88

takes place in a pupil who does understand this signal, which does not take place in the other pupil. The readiness to *assume* that some mental process occurs in the one which is not present in the other, is a nice illustration of what Wittgenstein was inclined to call an 'illness', and which he thought a philosopher should try to overcome. 'In philosophy one is in constant danger of producing a myth of symbolism, or of mental processes. Instead of simply saying what anyone knows and must admit' (*Z*, 211). A philosopher needs to fight hard against the many temptations to invent hidden states or processes. He needs to train himself to describe the grammar of language solely in terms of what 'lies open to view'. One constant tendency is to be 'bewitched' by the occurrence of *the same word* into thinking that its *meaning* remains the same – a tendency that can be overcome only by describing an array of different cases. 'A main cause of philosophical disease – one-sided diet: one nourishes one's thinking with only one kind of example' (*PI*, 593). The right kind of philosophical work is analogous to a therapy: 'A philosopher treats a question: like an illness' (*PI*, 255). But a philosopher must continually apply this therapy *to himself*. 'A philosopher is one who must heal in himself many diseases of the understanding, before he can arrive at the notions of common sense' (*VB*, p. 44). Wittgenstein found this a hard task for himself. 'How difficult it is for me to see, what *lies before my eyes!*' (*VB*, p. 39).

Wittgenstein was a serious man, and he took philosophy seriously. Although he sometimes compared the repetitious movements of philosophical thinking to an 'illness' of the understanding, he did not of course consider this as having anything like the deadly gravity of the moral and spiritual illness to which religion speaks. He could joke about philosophical problems, but not about religious ones. He created new methods for treating philosophical questions – and he employed them with confidence and power. But he did not think that he had any capacity for dealing with religious problems. He was convinced that religious commitment, at its deepest level, demands a complete turning round of the direction of one's life: but he surely felt that he could not, or would not, achieve that for himself.

The analogy between the sickness of the spirit that is of religious concern and the intellectual diseases that philosophy would like to heal must not be exaggerated. The analogy only means that in both cases something is wrong with us – on the other hand, in the way we live and feel and regard others; on the one hand, in the way we *think* when we encounter a philosophical question. About the latter,

Wittgenstein wrote; 'Our illness is this, to want to explain' (*RFM*, p. 333).

The fourth analogy is the following: Wittgenstein's conception of religious belief attached no value to intellectual proofs of God's existence, and very little value to theological formulations in general. He objected to the idea that Christianity is a 'doctrine'. For him the crucial aspect of serious religious feeling is the emphasis on 'changing one's life', 'amending one's ways', 'helping others'. For this position there is strong backing in both Jewish and Christian scriptures. Wittgenstein would have agreed with St James that 'Faith, without works, is dead.'

In Wittgenstein's post-*Tractatus* philosophical work a main current of his thinking is the insistence that our everyday concepts require a base of *acting, doing*, rather than reasoning or interpreting. This is one reason for his comparing our employment of language to playing games – for in games the players act and react. He says that instead of the weighing of grounds or of making inferences from evidence, 'it is our *acting*, which lies at the bottom of the language game' (*OC*, 204).

As an illustration, consider the way we use calculations. Sometimes we make mistakes in calculations, and have to correct them. Sometimes when the matter is important we will check a calculation several times, and perhaps ask others to check it. The important point, however, is that we bring this checking *to an end*: we *accept* the calculation, and act on it. We don't insist on still more checking: we terminate it. We don't justify our position by citing a rule, according to which a calculation that has been checked a certain number of times is correct: there is no such rule.

> In certain circumstances we consider a calculation to be sufficiently checked. What gives us a right to do so? Experience? May that not have deceived us? Somewhere we must finish with justification, and then there remains the proposition that we calculate like *this*.
>
> (*OC*, 212).

We *stop* checking. And of course if we did not stop, calculating would not exist. This is a splendid illustration of how a certain kind of *acting* is internal to a language-game. There might be an individual, a thorough sceptic, who refused to trust any calculation. We cannot prove him wrong – but despite this, we continue to accept calculations.

If someone supposed that *all* our calculations were uncertain and that we could rely on none of them (justifying himself by saying that mistakes are always possible), perhaps we would say he was crazy. But can we say he is in error? Does he not just react differently? We rely on calculations, he doesn't; we are sure, he isn't.

(*OC*, 217)

So there enters into even such a rational activity as calculation an action which is neither rational nor irrational – namely, the action of *taking* the calculation as *sufficiently* checked.

A leading problem of philosophy for many centuries has been the existence of other minds. Here it has seemed that it requires very sophisticated reasoning for a person to assure himself that those other 'walking and speaking figures' have minds and souls, just as he himself has. But in fact a normal human being does not have this doubt that those other creatures, which resemble him, might be automatons; nor does he go through subtle reasoning to remove the doubt. Wittgenstein dismisses the famous 'argument from analogy':

You say you take care of a man who groans, because experience has taught you that you yourself groan when you feel such-and-such. But since in fact you don't make any such inference, we can abandon the argument from analogy.

(*Z*, 537)

Instead of this supposed reasoning, which could only be carried out in language, Wittgenstein calls attention to natural actions and reactions that come *before* language and are not the result of *thought*:

It helps here to remember that it is a primitive reaction to tend to treat the part that hurts when someone else is in pain; and not merely when oneself is – and so to pay attention to the pain-behaviour of others, as one does *not* pay attention to one's own pain-behaviour.

(*Z*, 540)

The notion that those people around me might be automatons without minds or souls cannot get a foothold with me. I react to the expressions in their faces of fear, joy, interest – without the mediation of any reasoning. I smile back at someone who smiles at me; I draw back from an angry or threatening look. I do not *infer* that he is

91

angry, from his facial movements: I *see* the anger in his face, and I react to it.

These natural, instinctive, actions and reactions – rather than refined reasoning – lie at the base of our concept of a human being, of a being with mind and soul. The question of whether other people are automatons or whether they are genuine persons cannot arise for me. I do not persuade myself into the *belief* that those others have minds or souls. As Wittgenstein puts it: 'My attitude towards him is an attitude towards a soul. I am not of the *opinion* that he has a soul' (*PI*, p. 178).

Throughout his philosophical work Wittgenstein is attempting to locate the basis of our concepts in pre-linguistic, pre-rational actions and reactions. It is not from intuitions, nor convictions, nor any kind of reasoning, that our language-games emerge – but from 'our acting' (*OC*, 204).

Clearly, there is an analogy between Wittgenstein's view that our concepts rest on a basis of human actions and reactions, and his view that what is most fundamental in a religious life is not the affirming of creeds, nor even prayer and worship – but rather, doing *good deeds* – helping others in concrete ways, treating their needs as equal to one's own, opening one's heart to them, not being cold or contemptuous, but loving.

Thus, there are four analogies between Wittgenstein's conception of the grammar of language, and his view of what is paramount in a religious life. First, in both there is an end to explanation; second, in both there is an inclination to be amazed at the existence of something: third, into both there enters the notion of an 'illness'; fourth, in both, *doing, acting*, takes priority over intellectual understanding and reasoning.

Do these analogies present the meaning of Wittgenstein's remark that he saw philosophical problems from a religious point of view? I do not know. I cannot answer with any confidence. The analogies are there, and are worthy of reflection. But as an interpretation of Wittgenstein's surprising statement, they may be wide of the mark.

BIBLIOGRAPHY

The material used falls into three groups: I: writings and lectures by Wittgenstein; II: biographies, memoirs, and conversations of Wittgenstein; III: other books. Citations are in the text, and are either by remark number or page number.

I

Wittgenstein, Ludwig (1958a) *The Blue and Brown Books*, Oxford: Blackwell.

—— (1958b) *Philosophical Investigations*, 3rd edn, ed. G. E. M. Anscombe, tr. Rush Rhees and G. H. von Wright, New York: Macmillan.

—— (1965) 'A lecture on ethics', *Philosophical Review*, vol. 74, no.1, January.

—— (1967) *Zettel*, ed. G. E. M. Anscombe and G. H. von Wright, tr. G. E. M. Anscombe, Oxford: Blackwell.

—— (1969a) *On Certainty*, ed. G. E. M. Anscombe and G. H. von Wright, tr. Denis Paul and G. E. M. Anscombe, Oxford: Blackwell.

—— (1969b) *Tractatus Logico-Philosophicus*, tr. D. F. Pears and B. F. McGuinness, London: Routledge & Kegan Paul.

—— (1974) *Philosophical Grammar*, ed. Rush Rhees, tr. Anthony Kenny, Oxford: Blackwell.

—— (1978) *Remarks on The Foundations of Mathematics*, revised and expanded edn, ed. G. E. M. Anscombe, Rush Rhees and G. H. von Wright, Cambridge, Mass.: MIT Press.

—— (1979a) *Notebooks 1914–16*, 2nd edn, ed. G. H. von Wright and G. E. M. Anscombe, tr. G. E. M. Anscombe, Oxford: Blackwell.

—— (1979b) *Remarks on Frazer's Golden Bough*, ed. Rush Rhees, tr. A. C. Miles, Retford, Notts: Brynmill Press.

—— (1980) *Vermischte Bemerkungen* (Miscellaneous Remarks), ed. G. H. von Wright in collaboration with Heikki Nyman, tr. Peter Winch under the title *Culture and Value*, Oxford: Blackwell.

—— (1989) 'A lecture on freedom of the will', notes taken by Yorick Smythies, Cambridge 1946–7, *Philosophical Investigations*, vol. 12, no. 2, April.

II

Engelmann, Paul (1967) *Letters from Ludwig Wittgenstein with a Memoir*, ed. B. F. McGuinness, tr. L. Furtmüller, Oxford: Blackwell.

McGuinness, Brian (ed.) (1979) *Wittgenstein and the Vienna Circle*, conversations recorded by Friedrich Waismann, tr. Joachim Schulte and Brian McGuinness, Oxford: Blackwell.

—— (1988) *Wittgenstein: A Life*, vol. I: *Young Ludwig 1889–1921*, London: Duckworth.

Malcolm, Norman (1984) *Ludwig Wittgenstein: A Memoir*, with a 'Biographical sketch' by G. H. von Wright, 2nd edn, with Wittgenstein's letters to Malcolm, Oxford: Oxford University Press.

Rush Rhees (ed.) (1984) *Ludwig Wittgenstein, Personal Recollections*, Oxford: Oxford University Press.

III

Chomsky, Noam (1965) *Aspects of the Theory of Syntax*, Cambridge, Mass.: MIT Press.

—— (1972) *Language and Mind*, enlarged edn, New York: Harcourt Brace Jovanovich.

Hallett, Garth (1977) *A Companion to Wittgenstein's 'Philosophical Investigations'*, Ithaca and London: Cornell University Press.

Keegan, John (1978) *The Face of Battle*, Harmondsworth: Penguin Books.

Malcolm, Norman (1986) *Nothing Is Hidden*, Oxford: Blackwell. Published in paperback under the title *Wittgenstein: Nothing Is Hidden* (1988) Oxford: Blackwell.

DISCUSSION OF MALCOLM'S ESSAY

Peter Winch

In the elder days of art,
Builders wrought with greatest care
Each minute and unseen part,
For the gods are everywhere.

(Longfellow)

(This could serve me as a motto.) [1]

WHAT 'PROBLEMS'?

Malcolm begins his Chapter 2 as follows:

> Wittgenstein did much religious thinking: but religious thoughts do not figure in his detailed treatments of the philosophical problems. It would seem, therefore, that when he spoke of seeing those problems 'from a religious point of view', he did not mean that he conceived of them as religious problems, but instead that there was a similarity, or similarities, between his conception of philosophy and something that is characteristic of religious thinking.

This reading forms the basis of his interpretation.

Now, as quoted by Drury, Wittgenstein did not explicitly speak of *philosophical problems*. What he is supposed to have said is: 'I cannot help seeing *every problem* from a religious point of view.' Malcolm, in his Introduction, takes it as a matter of course that Wittgenstein was speaking here of philosophical problems. He writes:

'the problems' to which he was referring were not the problems of poverty, disease, unemployment, crime, brutality, racial prejudice, war. These problems oppress and bewilder mankind. Certainly they disturbed Wittgenstein. But he was not referring to them. The 'problems' he meant are *philosophical*: those very perplexities and confusions with which he grapples in the *Investigations*.

I find this misleading. First, the examples of problems with which Malcolm contrasts philosophical problems are both exiguous and strangely chosen. Although, of course, they are all problems that *can* be looked at from a religious point of view, they do not have to be and perhaps more frequently than not they are not generally seen in this way. Discussions of such problems do not loom large in Wittgenstein's writings or reported conversations, whereas there are other kinds of problem that we *do* find him discussing in a way it is natural to think of as religious or at least quasi-religious. For instance, the problem of how to live with something in one's past life of which one is ashamed; [2] the problem of how to conduct oneself in the face of death; [3] generally, the problem of how to live a decent life. [4] The point is not merely that these are kinds of question it is natural to think of when raising the issue of Wittgenstein's attitude to religion, but they are, some of them at least, questions much more directly relevant to the issue of the sense in which Wittgenstein may be thought to have seen *philosophical* problems 'from a religious point of view'. This can be seen from the passage from the Foreword Wittgenstein wrote to *Philosophical Remarks*, quoted by Drury: [5]

> I would like to say, 'this book is written to the glory of God', but nowadays this would be the trick of a cheat, i.e. it would not be correctly understood. It means the book was written in good will, and so far as it was not but was written from vanity etc., the author would wish to see it condemned. He can not make it more free of these impurities than he is himself.

Second, I find misleading the *exclusive* terms in which Malcolm states the alternatives: *either* the large socio-political problems he mentions *or* philosophical problems. Certainly, Wittgenstein must have meant to *include* philosophical problems in what he said to Drury, but not to the exclusion of everything, or indeed anything, else. This is not a minor matter. Malcolm's essay rests on the assumption that Wittgenstein meant that he saw an *analogy* between philosophical and religious problems and his discussion is carried out on that supposition. But the supposition is only plausible as long as we take Wittgenstein to be speaking of philosophical problems in an exclusive way. We may perhaps allow that he was singling out his attitude to philosophical problems for special attention, but there is no reason to think that he was not also expressing an attitude to many other sorts of problem as well. Once this is acknowledged, it becomes almost senseless, or at least implausible in the highest degree, to suppose he was talking of an analogy between philosophical and religious problems. Are we also to say for instance that he saw an analogy between religious problems and problems of decency in one's manner of life? If we do so, we are in danger of losing our grip on any manageable question.

By most people's standards Wittgenstein was obsessively precise about the way he expressed himself. Now he did not, of course, actually speak to Drury of seeing an 'analogy' between philosophical and religious problems, but of 'seeing every problem from a religious point of view'. Add to this that he *did* frequently speak of there being analogies between one type of problem and another, and he even spoke of an analogy between *philosophical* problems and *aesthetic* problems. [6] 'The queer resemblance between a philosophical investigation (perhaps especially in mathematics) and an aesthetic one. (E.g. what is bad about this garment, how it should be, etc.)' In this case I think he clearly did have in mind something technically methodological; namely that, like philosophical questions, aesthetic problems are not illuminated by theorizing – especially psychological theorizing, but by the drawing of analogies, seeing what is problematic against a variety of different backgrounds and so on. And this view is fleshed out through many examples which Wittgenstein discusses of particular aesthetic questions. I find nothing of the sort in what he writes about religious questions. [7]

Considerations like these make me think it is perhaps a mistake to try to construe Wittgenstein's remark to Drury as proposing an *analogy* between philosophical and religious questions. I shall return to this point at a later stage, when I shall also try to say something in more detail about the precise points of analogy to which Malcolm draws attention in his concluding chapter. I shall myself conclude by offering some tentative suggestions about an alternative way of construing Wittgenstein's remark.

MALCOLM ON WITTGENSTEIN'S PHILOSOPHY

First, however, I must turn my attention to the longest part of Malcolm's essay: his general discussion of Wittgenstein's philosophy. This is a succinct and vigorous discussion which brings together and supplements many issues treated by Malcolm more extensively in earlier works.

Tractatus

The main philosophical focus of Malcolm's attempt to interpret Wittgenstein's view of the relation between philosophy and religion is of course not on the *Tractatus* so much as on the later works, especially the *Philosophical Investigations*. It is not, or should not be, a matter of controversy that the *Philosophical Investigations* is in large part a reaction against the *Tractatus* and this is something on which Malcolm places a great deal of emphasis. Hence, if we are to assess his reading of the *Philosophical Investigations* it is important that we also come to terms with *what* exactly it is against which he thinks the later work is reacting. Malcolm regards the *Tractatus* as a grand exercise in explanatory metaphysics, an attempt to 'explain' language by showing how its possibility and structure flow from the structure of 'the world'. [8]

It is characteristic of Malcolm's reading that he puts little emphasis on the very last propositions of the *Tractatus*, especially 6.53–7. In these passages, as is well known, Wittgenstein distances himself from the sentences he has written up to that point to the extent of saying that the reader will not have understood him if he does not recognize those sentences as nonsense (*unsinnig*).

> 6.54 My propositions serve as elucidations in the following way: anyone who understands me eventually recognizes them as nonsensical, when he has used them – as steps – to climb up beyond them. (He must, so to speak, throw away the ladder after he has climbed up it.)
>
> He must transcend these propositions, and then he will see the world aright.

The prominent position of these remarks at the culmination of the book seems clearly to demand that they should be taken very seriously, and certainly not as a rhetorical flourish that can safely be ignored. Wittgenstein himself insisted on their importance in various places – for instance in a letter complaining about the use Carnap had made of the *Tractatus*. [9] The best case I know for thinking that they are to be taken *au pied de la lettre* is that made by James Conant. [10] Of course these remarks have given endless trouble to commentators who have taken Wittgenstein to be saying on the one hand that what he writes in the *Tractatus* is to be *understood*, but at the same time recognized as *nonsense*. As against this Conant points out that Wittgenstein does not speak of understanding his *sentences*, but of understanding *him*. Once this distinction is put in the foreground it becomes clear that to understand Wittgenstein is precisely to understand that he is offering sentences which he knows to be nonsense. We, his readers, are to understand his purpose in doing this: namely to articulate the metaphysical temptations to which we are subject and show that they lead to nonsense. In this way we are to be cured of our temptations.

The point is of course to recognize the purpose with which he is doing this: he is, as it were, trying to articulate for us, his readers, the metaphysical temptations to which we are subject in such a way as to show us that they lead us into nonsense and thereby to enable us to overcome them. [11] This puts the relation between the *Tractatus* and the *Philosophical Investigations* in quite a different light from Malcolm's interpretation. The point of the later work is not to combat a metaphysical theory maintained in the earlier, but to execute the work of combating such theories more effectively than was done in the *Tractatus*.

There is a further feature of Malcolm's discussion of the *Tractatus* which needs to be brought into the picture before we turn to later developments in Wittgenstein's thinking, namely the treatment there of laws in natural science. Malcolm points out that according to the *Tractatus* phenomena are not *explained* by natural laws. In general I have no criticism to make of his treatment of this theme. I think he is right in thinking that it is a matter concerning which Wittgenstein never changed his mind in any fundamental way – though certainly his thinking about it became enriched and took new turns as his general philosophical understanding developed. The only point here about which I have reservations is the impression given that what Wittgenstein writes about explanation in the context of natural science is somehow on all fours with his views on the inappropriateness of explanatory theories in philosophy. This has some importance in the overall context of Malcolm's essay, one purpose of which is to show that there is a general attitude to explanation in

Wittgenstein's thinking, which makes itself apparent in a number of different contexts. I shall shortly try to show that this leads Malcolm to give a somewhat false emphasis, in his account of Wittgenstein's use of 'language-games', to the position that language-games 'cannot be explained'. He sometimes tends to overlook the very different issues that are at stake in various of the contexts in which Wittgenstein insists that 'explanation has an end'. The running together of the treatment in the *Tractatus* of natural laws in science with Wittgenstein's later discussions of the inappropriateness of explanatory theories in philosophy is an example of a similar tendency to underplay differences. I shall be suggesting later, more relevantly to our central topic, that Malcolm's main thesis about the alleged analogies Wittgenstein saw between philosophy and religion is yet another example.

Chomsky: language and thought in the *Tractatus*

Malcolm's treatment of Chomsky in Chapter 4 belongs with his discussion of the *Tractatus*. In the overall argument of the essay, however, it serves to link the discussion of the *Tractatus* with the treatment of themes which he deals with in subsequent chapters. Chomsky's theories of language certainly exercised him a great deal and I think he was in a way incensed that they should have exerted such an influence given, as he was convinced to be the case, that the pretensions of any such theory had been revealed as hollow by Wittgenstein's work, especially in the *Philosophical Investigations*.

I share this conviction, but think Malcolm was wrong to suppose that Wittgenstein himself had put forward any such view as his own in the *Tractatus*. The truth, I believe, is that Wittgenstein's concern, already at that time, was to try to make clear that the temptation to theorize in this way, which he well understood, is the result of nothing but confusion.

Malcolm rests much weight on *Tractatus* 4.002. He takes the statement: 'Language disguises thoughts. And it does so in such a way that we cannot infer the form of the clothed thought from the outward form of the clothing' to refer to the relation between spoken language and thought *in the sense of something inner and psychological – a mental process.* [12] Of course Wittgenstein was well aware of the temptation to regard thought in this way, but, as I read his treatment, he quite explicitly rejects such a view. *Tractatus* 3.11 reads: 'We use the perceptible sign of a proposition (spoken or written, etc.) as a projection of a possible situation. The method of projection is to think of the sense of the proposition.' I have used the Pears/McGuinness translation which (unlike C. K. Ogden's version[13]) obscures the ambiguity of the German in the last sentence: 'Die Projektionsmethode ist das Denken des Satz-Sinnes.' Taken by itself this can be read as saying *either*: 'thinking the sense of the proposition consists of the method of projection' *or* 'the method of projection consists of thinking the sense of the proposition'. Malcolm of course takes it in the second of these ways.

I say that 'taken by itself' it has this ambiguity. But in fact it does not stand alone. It is the culmination of a long argument which we can take to begin at *Tractatus* 2.1. The argument develops the notion of a *picture* as a constellation of elements constructed according to a given 'method of a projection' which gives it a relation to a 'possible state of affairs'. The method of projection confers a 'form of representation' on what thus becomes the picture and, because one aspect of any form of representation is *logical* form, every picture, whatever else it may be, is *at the same time* a logical picture (*T*, 2.182). Proposition 3 then formally introduces the term 'thought' explicitly in terms of the logical notions developed in those preceding propositions: 'A logical picture of the facts is a thought.' The discussion that then follows continues to insist on the *logical* character of the notion of a 'thought'; there is absolutely no mention here of psychical, or mental, processes. The last sentence of proposition 3.11 *cannot* mean 'Thinking the sense of the proposition is what the method of projection is', since, first, the concept of a method of projection has already been explained at that point in quite different – logical – terms; and, second, the concept of a thought has been introduced on the back of that very same explanation. The earlier *Prototractatus* makes this structure even clearer, I think. It contains two further propositions: '3.12 The method of projection is the way in which the sentential sign is applied. 3.13 Applying the sentential sign is thinking its sense.'[14]

In fact what is presented at this point in the *Tractatus* is a skeletal and undeveloped precursor of the position magnificently developed in the *Philosophical Investigations*, according to which notions like understanding and meaning (in the sense of meaning something by what you say) are not to be understood as psychological notions but rather as logical notions, an interpretation that is pivotal to the whole argument of the *Philosophical Investigations* and which is explicitly said to be so at the end of §81 of that work.[15]

101

None of this of course in any way damages Malcolm's critique of Chomsky. On the contrary, rightly understood, I should say it strengthens it, by showing that part of Wittgenstein's critique of the foundations of a theory like Chomsky's was already available in 1918.

Philosophical Investigations

In Chapter 5 Malcolm discusses various topics which are treated in Wittgenstein's *Philosophical Investigations* and elsewhere in his later writings. These discussions are often illuminating in themselves, but their role in the overall strategy of the book is to bring out how, throughout Wittgenstein's treatment of these various questions, a pervasive common attitude to explanation is discernible. Chapter 6 is an explicit discussion of this attitude to explanation.

I have no doubt at all that Malcolm is right in discerning such a pervasive attitude to explanation in Wittgenstein's writing. All the same, I find myself profoundly uneasy at the *kind* of emphasis that he gives it. This is of course a matter which is of central importance to his treatment of the analogy he thinks Wittgenstein saw between philosophy and religion. It is something about which I must try to get clear.

In Chapter 2 Malcolm notes the great diversity of activities over which the word 'explanation' ranges. He focuses particularly on the difference between the sense in which natural scientists can be said to search for explanations and the sense in which this can be said of what philosophers have characteristically engaged in. Whereas natural scientists explore the reasons, or causes, for the occurrence of various kinds of events,

> philosophy is not an empirical science. But from antiquity it has been dominated by a tradition of explanation. Philosophers have been fascinated and perplexed by concepts, such as *beauty, justice, knowledge*. They have wanted to find out what justice or beauty or knowledge *is*. Their concentration, however, was not on doings or happenings in the world, but on the *meaning* of these words. When you say that you 'know' this or that, what are you *saying*? Usually the concentration was on *truth-conditions*. When you say that you *know* that so-and-so, what are the necessary and sufficient conditions that must be satisfied in order for your assertion to be true? If a philosopher could spell out those conditions he would be giving a

definition of the meaning of 'know'. He would have given a logical analysis, or a philosophical analysis, of *knowledge*. This would be an 'explanation' of what knowledge is, what it consists of. It is a different form of explanation than occurs in chemistry or physics, and a different kind of analysis: but still it would be analysis and explanation.

I do not want to quarrel with any of this as far as it goes. What is mainly *lacking*, I think, is any account of the kinds of puzzle that have led philosophers to think explanations along these lines called for. Their reasons for wanting analyses in terms of necessary and sufficient conditions have been connected with a certain view of what logic requires of a significant utterance. It has seemed to them that the logical consequences that can be drawn from such an utterance must be precisely determined by the *meaning* which it bears at the time at which it is made; and that, furthermore, that meaning, i.e. all the necessary and sufficient conditions of the use of the utterance, must be intended, *meant*, by the utterer at the time of the utterance, since otherwise the utterer will be at full liberty to accept or refuse a given consequence at random and no one will ever know with certainty what anyone (including him or herself) is actually saying. And that would amount to a situation in which no one was genuinely saying anything.

I have sketched this point roughly here mainly for two reasons. First, because it is important to see what *type* of explanation Wittgenstein finds it necessary to warn philosophers away from seeking in the context of their problems, namely explanations which provide users of the language with a justification for using words in the way they do. Second, because Wittgenstein's treatments of philosophical puzzles go far beyond pointing out that ultimate explanations in terms of necessary and sufficient conditions are not in fact for the most part available in the contexts where philosophers seek them: *most* of his attention is devoted rather to accurate diagnosis of the difficulties which give rise to such a search and an attempt to show that these difficulties are in the end the result of confusions. Wittgenstein never thought that convincing the philosopher that explanations come to an end would be enough to stop the obsessional insistence on asking unanswerable questions. The real work that had to be done was to make clear the misunderstanding from which that insistence arose. Arriving at clarity concerning the limits of explanation would be, at most, a stage on the way.

I have thought it worth making this point because Malcolm sometimes gives the impression that Wittgenstein's main purpose in criticizing our search for explanations in philosophy was to get us to see the futility of this because 'then we can focus on the phenomena themselves, and even be awakened to a kind of *wonder* at their existence'.

This is particularly important in the context of Malcolm's overall argument, since he does want to ascribe a quasi-religious significance to the wonder that Wittgenstein himself often expressed at the unending variety of human forms of life. I think there is some plausibility in thinking of Wittgenstein's attitude in this way, in some contexts at least. But I think there is no basis for any suggestion that he in any way saw the purpose of his philosophical investigations as directed towards the awakening of such a religious wonder. Perhaps Malcolm did not want to suggest this; but occasional remarks somewhat give that impression.

A more serious point is the following. At the end of Chapter 6 Malcolm writes:

> Wittgenstein's emphasized theme that reasons, justifications, explanations come to an end ... means that these come to an end *somewhere*. Where is that? It is at the *existence* of the language-games and the associated forms of life. There is where explanation has reached its limit. There reasons stop.

I think it is a fact worthy of note that Wittgenstein does *not* characteristically follow a reminder that explanations come to an end with any such general questions as '*Where* do they end?' And I believe that to ask the question is to betray a misunderstanding. Spinoza thought that because explanations have to come to an end there must be something which has no further explanation, a *causa sui*. But Wittgenstein's point is not at all like that – it is a *criticism* of such an outlook. He does not think that explanations come to an end with something that is intrinsically beyond further explanation. They come to an end for a variety of quite contingent and pragmatic reasons, perhaps because of a practical need for action, perhaps because the puzzlement which originally prompted the search for explanation has evaporated (for one reason or another).

It is misleading to say that 'Wittgenstein regarded the language-games, and their associated forms of life, as beyond explanation.' Language-games are not a phenomenon that Wittgenstein had discovered with the peculiar property that their existence cannot be explained!

Malcolm appears at this stage in his argument to have forgotten his own earlier observation about the great diversity of different kinds of explanation. He writes, early in Chapter 7,

> Philosophy can observe a complicated linguistic practice and describe how one movement in it is related to another. But philosophy cannot explain why the practice exists: nor can the 'hard' sciences of physics, chemistry, biology; nor the 'soft' sciences of psychology, sociology, anthropology.

But this seems to me neither generally true in itself, nor implied by anything Wittgenstein wrote. He was concerned with the peculiar pseudo-sense in which *philosophers* seek 'explanation'. His criticism did not terminate in pointing to the existence of something that happens to be beyond the reach of explanation; the force of the criticism lay in his exposure of the confusions involved in the search itself and in the puzzlement that gives rise to it. The concept of a language-game has to be understood as a logical instrument in the service of that exposure. It is relevant to remind ourselves at this point of Wittgenstein's insistence that invented language-games are as good for this purpose as actual ones: indeed, at some points they are better. His appeal is to be understood not as: 'Look, here is something that can't be explained', but rather, 'Look at things from this point of view; then you will see that the difficulties that you are trying to deal with are not going to be dealt with through any sort of explanation of the sort you are seeking.' A superb succinct example of a typical technique of his is the following passage:

> Well, if everything speaks for an hypothesis and nothing against it – is it then certainly true? One may designate it as such. – But does it certainly agree with reality, with the facts? – With this question you are already going round in a circle. [16]

The argument is not: 'You are trying to find an explanation for something which of its nature cannot be explained'; but rather: 'Look at how you are arguing, don't you see that this way of thinking is not going to get you anywhere? You think you need an explanation, but your real difficulty is one that needs a quite different sort of treatment.'

Furthermore, as far as the 'hard' and 'soft' sciences (as distinct from philosophy) are concerned, Wittgenstein's point was not, I believe, that language-games are intrinsically beyond the power of these sciences to provide explanations, but rather that any explanation they might offer would turn out to be quite uninteresting and useless *as far as the philosopher's characteristic puzzlement is concerned*. He recognized, of course, that this puzzlement is not confined to 'professional' philosophers, but may be experienced by 'hard' and 'soft' scientists alike as well, and that in such a case it is quite on the cards that a scientist will offer an explanation of the kind with which he or she is familiar in the belief that this will provide a solution to the puzzlement. That would be a confusion. But this does nothing to show that explanations may not be found by such scientists which provide perfectly good answers to other kinds of question. For instance there are many cases in which historians, anthropologists or linguists give well-founded explanations of the existence of this or that practice. Why ever not?! The important question *for us* to ask is: what relevance would such explanations have to the resolution of *philosophical* difficulties?

I confess that I am just not sure how deep these criticisms of Malcolm go. Often enough he shows himself very well aware of points like those I have tried to make. But he does also sometimes write in ways that give one pause. This is connected with the impression, very widespread particularly amongst psychologists acquainted with his work, as well as amongst philosophers, that he is *anti-scientific*. I am sure that as a general charge this is unjustified. For instance, in his book *Memory and Mind* [17] (which I find not only one of his best works but the best existing philosophical treatment of its subject) the distinction between the kind of explanation that lies quite legitimately within the province of a psychologist's investigation and the kind that misunderstands the difference between psychological and philosophical issues is pretty clearly drawn and by and large consistently observed. The hostility that it has nevertheless engendered amongst some psychologists is no doubt due to the fact that the very making of this distinction threatens the unrealistic pretensions some of them have for their subject.

But in the essay with which we are now concerned I think Malcolm is not as cautious as he needs to be. For instance, in Chapter 4 he offers an excellent, trenchant, criticism of Chomsky's form of 'explanation' of how a child comes to be able to speak its mother tongue. The criticism focuses on the confusions involved in the way Chomsky raises the questions, namely – roughly – in terms of some task which the child has to figure out a method of accomplishing. But in his further reflections on the subject Malcolm begins to write as though there are no intelligible questions to be raised at all concerning the nature, or causal conditions, of the ability of a child to learn to speak. Consider the following:

> Suppose I was travelling in Africa and met a person who, for some reason or other, thought I was French. He is impressed by my ability to speak English, and asks me how it came about that I have such a good command of that language. My reply would be: 'English is my native tongue.' This would be an explanation – *for* that person who asked his question only because he wrongly believed that English was not my native language. Once that error is corrected, he will no longer ask how I learned English. . . . That is not a possible question for him, or for me, or for anyone else.

And at the end of the chapter:

> If someone explains his proficiency in English by informing us that he grew up in an English-speaking community, this is not a 'superficial' explanation. There is no 'deeper' explanation. This is an example of where explanation has come to an end.

Malcolm is no doubt quite right in pointing out that, in the circumstances he described (in the first of these quotations), 'explanation has come to an end'. But that fact is a function of those circumstances. The circumstances of Chomsky's inquiry are very different, as is the question he raises. He does not ask: how did this particular person come to speak English? He asks: how does anyone come to speak his native tongue? I think it is likely that Chomsky was confused about the relation between these two questions, taking the one to be simply a generalization of the other. In fact the question can be understood in many different ways. For instance it may arise as a result of comparing two children, one of whom does learn the language of his or her community while the other does not. Why the difference? The answer might be in terms, for instance, of the development of the one child's brain, as contrasted with that of the other; it might be answered in terms of differences in sociological or psychological circumstances in the two cases. And these answers may lead to further investigations. The question of whether explanation has or has not come to an end depends on the kind of question that is being asked.

I think that Malcolm might have made this sort of point more explicitly – both here and in other works. It would have pre-empted much criticism and might have made some members of the audience he wanted to reach more receptive to what he was saying.

MALCOLM ON WITTGENSTEIN AND RELIGIOUS BELIEF

In considering what Wittgenstein meant by seeing problems 'from a religious point of view', it would seem natural for us to raise the question of what particular sort of religion, or religious belief, he had in mind. However, there are certain difficulties here which are suggested by an important passage in which Drury discussed Wittgenstein's relation to Pascal.

> For Pascal there was only one true religion, Christianity: only one true form of Christianity, Catholicism; only one true expression of Catholicism, Port Royal. Now although Wittgenstein would have respected this narrowness for its very intensity, such exclusiveness was foreign to his way of thinking. He was early influenced by William James' *Varieties of Religious Experience*. This book he told me had helped him greatly. And if I am not mistaken the category of *Varieties* continued to play an important part in his thinking.

> WITTGENSTEIN: The way in which people have had [18] to express their religious beliefs differ enormously. All genuine expressions of religion are wonderful even those of the most savage peoples.

> In the 'Remarks on Frazer's Golden Bough' he writes: 'Was St. Augustine mistaken then, when he called on God on every page of the *Confessions*? Well – one might say – if he was not mistaken, then the Buddhist holy man, or some other, whose religion expresses quite different notions, surely was. But none of them was making a mistake except where he was putting forward a theory.' [19]

It is clear from this, as indeed from many other passages in which Wittgenstein *contrasts* religion and theory – good examples of which Malcolm quotes in his Chapter 1, that the phrase 'from a religious point of view' cannot be interpreted in terms of any particular theological doctrine.

This brings into focus a point which would anyway have to be faced, namely that there is much unclarity concerning the kind of terms we should use in distinguishing between a 'religious' and a 'non-religious' point of view. The difficulty is made more complicated by the fact – amply illustrated in James's *Varieties*[20] – that the great diversity within the category of religious faith is not merely a *confessional* diversity. Even within a given confession different believers have vastly diverse forms of religious sensibility. And these different forms of diversity criss-cross in bewilderingly complex ways.

For instance, as Malcolm shows himself to be well aware, by no means all religious believers take the same view as Malcolm and Wittgenstein of the relation between talking of 'the will of God' and acknowledging that certain kinds of demand for *explanation* are out of place. Indeed the Book of Job itself makes this clear in the contrast between Job after he has reached enlightenment and his 'comforters'. And if we want an example from nearer home, we need only look at the repeated and continuing attempts to justify the ways of God to men on the part of believing philosophers and of theologians.

However, as far as we are concerned the position is not hopeless. We are not in the business of trying to arrive at a definition, or even a characterization, of religious belief that would cover all cases. We need only consider the forms of religious belief towards which Wittgenstein himself was most sympathetic or felt himself most inclined. There is plenty of material for this purpose: in, for instance, many of the remarks in *Culture and Value*, in his war diaries, in his own academic discussions of religious belief[21] and in the reports of those who knew him. Malcolm himself offers a very useful selection from this material in Chapter 1.

For instance, the idea of a last judgment on one's life clearly meant a great deal to Wittgenstein's view of his own life. He was also inclined to think of life as a 'gift' and hence as something for which one can be grateful, but as something too that imposes inescapable obligations. He recognized that certain things could not be achieved just by his own efforts, but required help, or 'light' from above, from 'the spirit'. And so on. These are all attitudes which, in different religions, are set in specific doctrinal contexts. *In* such contexts there is no doubt that they constitute religious attitudes. But it is also natural to regard them in this way, even when they are not connected in the person's life with specific confessional commitments and when, from the point of view of developed theological doctrine, they are inchoate. It is natural too, I think, to regard someone with such attitudes as having a religious sensibility of a kind one does not find in everyone, not even necessarily in the most ethically serious of people. Indeed, in some people ethical seriousness manifests itself precisely in a certain kind of *opposition* to such attitudes. In trying to make sense of Wittgenstein's claim to see problems 'from a religious point of view' we must consider his attitudes in the context of parameters such as these.

Four analogies?

As we have seen, Malcolm approaches the task of interpreting this phrase in terms of possible *analogies* that Wittgenstein may have seen between philosophy and religion. In his Chapter 7 he suggests four such:

1 An analogy in respect of an attitude towards explanation.
2 An analogy between a kind of religious wonder at the existence of the world, of which Wittgenstein spoke in his 'Lecture on ethics' and a kind of wonder expressed in his philosophical writings 'at the existence of the various language-games and their contained forms of action and reaction'.
3 An analogy between the religious attitude of regarding oneself as radically imperfect or 'sick' and the idea that philosophical puzzlement is a symptom of a 'disease' of our thinking.
4 An analogy between Wittgenstein's insistence that religion (Christianity at least) is not so much a 'doctrine' as a 'changing of one's life' and his post-*Tractatus* insistence that our everyday concepts require a base of *acting, doing* – rather than reasoning or interpreting.

I will comment on the first of these point at some length and then more briefly on the others.

Religion, philosophy and explanation

In the section on *Philosophical Investigations* (above), I was critical of the account, sometimes suggested in Malcolm's essay, of the role played by Wittgenstein's attitude to explanation in his philosophy. But I do not want to deny that Wittgenstein was critical of a certain kind of obsession with explanation no doubt especially prevalent in our present age. This critical attitude plays an important role in many of his most characteristic philosophical arguments and it has its analogues in his treatment of other important issues outside philosophy, including religion. This is manifest throughout those writings – I think from all periods – which concern religion in one way or another.

Many of the passages Malcolm cites bring this out very well. But he wants to say more. Having noted that for many people religion is hardly something to be taken seriously at all, and for others it is positively harmful to human development, he continues:

> Yet there are many people, even in this technological and materialistic age, who observe religious practices – praying to God for help, asking Him for forgiveness, thanking Him for the blessings of this life – and who thereby gain comfort and strength, hope and cheerfulness. Many of these people would have no understanding of what it would *mean* to provide a 'rational justification' for their religious belief – nor do they feel a need for it. Many would regard their faith as itself an undeserved *gift* from God. When overwhelmed by calamity, they arrive at a kind of reconciliation, once they come to feel that their sufferings are God's will. They would see no sense in asking *why* God willed these troubles to occur. To speak of God's will is, for them, an end to explanation. When Wittgenstein said that all he wanted was that his philosophical work 'should be God's will', he would certainly have considered any question as to *why* it should be God's will as nonsensical.
>
> The analogy to philosophy is that reasons, justifications, explanations, reach a terminus in the language-games and their internally related forms of human life.

For proper evaluation of Malcolm's thesis it is important to distinguish two points among those that are being made here. On the one hand it is said that the expression of religious belief is itself a language-game for which it makes no sense to ask for an explanation or rational justification. On the other hand it is said that, for a religious believer, a reference to God's will is 'an end to explanation'.

As far as the first of these points is concerned, it is misleading to speak of any *analogy* to philosophy, since the point itself is simply a philosophical one. Malcolm has already, in the body of his essay, claimed that it is characteristic of *all* language-games that they are, in this sense, beyond explanation. In so far as the expression of religious belief, therefore, is treated as itself a language-game, then of course it too in the same sense must be beyond explanation. But in this respect it will be no different from, say, scientific investigation, which, to be sure, *seeks* explanations but is not itself to be explained!

Malcolm makes the further remark at this point that a believer may well regard his or her religious faith as a *gift from God.* Of course, this does add a new religious dimension, but it does not support an analogy between religion and philosophy. A philosopher who accepts Wittgenstein's way of speaking of language-games as a point at which explanations come to an end is in no way committed to the further step that these language-games are a gift from God! And this holds true even where the language-game in question is one in which religious belief is expressed. Some philosophers may indeed think like this; perhaps Wittgenstein did. In so far as he did, then, no doubt, this would have to be regarded as connected in an important way with his saying that he could not help seeing problems from a religious point of view; but it would not at all show that he saw any *analogy* between philosophy and religion.

The second point is twofold: that for a believer – at least for a believer of a certain kind – to say that something is God's will is not itself to offer an explanation; and for him, moreover, it will make no sense to ask *why* it should be God's will. These are claims about a particular feature of a certain kind of religious language-game. As such they are themselves philosophical points, though points *about* religious belief. If one is to speak of any 'analogy' between philosophy and religion at this point, then, I suppose a case must be made for saying that the readiness to come to rest at a certain point and say, as it were, explanation stops here, plays a role within religion (regarding references to God's will) analogous to the role such a readiness plays in philosophy, as practised by Wittgenstein (regarding references to language-games). In fact Malcolm does say something like this: he thinks that in religion the phrase 'It is God's will' has 'a similar logical force' to the phrase. 'That's how it is', as used in philosophy. Both expressions 'tell us to stop asking "Why?" and instead to *accept a fact*'.

It seems to me that when the point is spelled out in this way, it looks problematic. The following important passage written by Wittgenstein in 1950 is relevant to this point.

If someone who believes in God looks round and asks 'Where does everything I see come from?', 'Where does all this come from?', he is *not* craving for a causal explanation; and his question gets it point from being the expression of a certain craving. He is, namely, expressing an attitude to all explanations. But how is this manifested in his life?

The attitude that's in question is that of taking a certain matter seriously and then, beyond a certain point, no longer regarding it as serious, but maintaining that something else is even more important.

Someone may for instance say it's a very grave matter that such and such a man should have died before he could complete a certain piece of work; and yet, in another sense, this is not what matters. At this point one uses the words 'in a deeper sense'.

Actually I should like to say that in this case too the *words* you utter or what you think as you utter them are not what matters, so much as the difference they make at various points in your life. How do I know that two people mean the same when each says he believes in God? And just the same goes for belief in the Trinity. A theology which insists on the use of *certain particular* words and phrases, and outlaws others, does not make anything clearer (Karl Barth). It gesticulates with words, as one might say, because it wants to say something and does not know how to express it. *Practice* gives the words their sense. [22]

Wittgenstein's question how the attitude to explanation to which he is referring shows itself in a person's life is a warning against too hasty a comparison with attitudes in other contexts that may be similarly expressed. And the whole passage spells out that warning. '*Practice* gives the words their sense.' And the practice associated with giving up the demand for explanation in philosophy bears little comparison with the giving up of the demand for explanation in religion, despite the similar words with which we may, in part at least, describe them.

I want to make one last point in a similar sense. As Malcolm brings out, the attitude of acceptance of one's fate as 'the will of God', an attitude which neither pretends to provide any explanation of that fate nor seeks to find one, characteristically goes along with an attitude of *gratitude* for life. But acceptance of things as they are, and recognition that, beyond a certain point, no explanation can significantly be required as to *why* they are like that, certainly need not be accompanied by gratitude. Another passage describes a diametrically opposed attitude.

> 'The cussedness of things.' – An unnecessary anthropomorphism. We might speak of the *world* as malicious; we could easily imagine the Devil had created the world, or part of it. And it is *not* necessary to imagine the evil spirit intervening in particular situations; everything can happen 'according to the laws of nature'; it is just that the whole scheme of things will be aimed at evil from the very start. But man exists in this world, where things break, slide about, cause every imaginable mischief. And of course he is one such thing himself. – The 'cussedness' of things is a stupid anthropomorphism. Because the truth is much graver than this fiction. [23]

The reference to the Devil here is no more an explanation than is a reference to the will of God. Indeed, the 'stupid anthro–pomorphism' consists precisely in thinking an explanation is needed in each particular case instead of simply saying: the world is the work of the Devil. Someone else again might simply say: 'That's how things are', without reference either to God or the Devil. We have throughout to bear in mind Wittgenstein's reminder, in a passage I quoted earlier, that the significance of these expressions depends not so much on the *words* used as on the difference their use makes in the user's life.

Suppose one compares these various cases. I think it is clear that quite different similarities and difference may strike one according to one's point of view. One might want to contrast the reference to the 'cussedness of things' with *all* the other cases on the grounds that it is the only attitude which takes any explanation of the particular case to be required at all. Or one might want to single out the reference to the will of God as the only one that expresses a religious attitude; or one might want to single out 'That's just how things are' as the only attitude genuinely 'free of all superstition'.

I really see no grounds for thinking that Wittgenstein would have singled out the *religious* attitude as showing a particularly close analogy to his own *philosophical* attitude. There is another, more positive, point to be made, however, that is related to Malcolm's talk about an 'analogy', though hardly to be expressed in those terms. Obstacles in the way of religious belief are legion and of many different kinds. Some such obstacles, though of course by no means all, are intellectual in nature, and of these some are thrown up by the particular intellectual culture in which we now live. Malcolm's reference, in an earlier quotation, to 'this technological and materialistic age' points in the direction of certain such obstacles. I think it is undeniable that the habit of asking certain kinds of question and of constantly seeking explanations,.which is one important feature of this culture, often plays a certain role here. It can for instance lead to a belief that an attitude to explanation like the one Wittgenstein describes [24] is somehow 'unscientific' – or even 'anti-scientific'. Such an intellectual stance can work in various ways in relation to an individual's religious belief or lack of it. It may influence the direction such belief takes. For instance, the kind of religious belief that seems to lie behind much contemporary academic work in philosophy of religion, with its emphasis on 'rationality' and 'justification' is clearly very different from that to which both Wittgenstein and Malcolm attach importance. Or again such an intellectual stance may form a barrier to anyone's having any sort of religious belief at all, or even to taking it seriously.

It is entirely possible that a study of Wittgenstein's treatment of the constant search for explanation that is typical of so much of our lives, his insistence that 'explanations come to an end', will have a liberating effect on some people and enable them to take certain religious attitudes seriously in a way they would not have been able to before. Of course, that would still be a very long way indeed from *acquiring* any sort of religious faith, but it could open the way to it.

There are other aspects of Wittgenstein's philosophical work too which *may* sometimes work in the same direction: for instance the searching discussions of the relation between name and object which run through so much of the *Philosophical Investigations*. [25]

I do not however think that Wittgenstein would have taken facts like these as having much to do with his 'seeing every problem from a religious point of view'; nor do I think that he would have been right to do so. For one thing, clarity about such matters as these could just as well lead to a *weakening* of religious faith in some people. 'If that is what religious faith comes to', some may think, 'it doesn't have the kind of importance I thought it had.' Wittgenstein made various remarks that have a bearing on this. For instance:

> The solution of philosophical problems can be compared with a gift in a fairy tale: in the magic castle it appears enchanted and if you look at it outside in daylight it is nothing but an ordinary bit of iron (or something of the sort). [26]

And also:

> The mathematician too can wonder at the miracles (the crystal) of nature; but can he do so once a problem has arisen about *what* it actually is he is contemplating? Is it really possible as long as the object that he finds astonishing and gazes at with awe is *shrouded* in a philosophical fog?
>
> I could imagine somebody might admire not only real trees, but also the shadows or reflections that they cast, taking them too for trees. But once he has told himself that these are not really trees after all and has come to be puzzled at what they are, or at how they are related to trees, his admiration will have suffered a rupture that will need healing. [27]

A sense of wonder

The second analogy Malcolm sees is between the sense of 'wonder at the existence of the world' that Wittgenstein referred to in his 'Lecture on ethics' of 1929 [28] and what Malcolm calls 'a kind of wonder at the existence of the various language-games and their contained forms of human action and reaction'. His discussion of this is somewhat perfunctory. Wittgenstein's attitude of 'wonder' at the language-games he describes in his philosophy is, Malcolm writes, 'not a religious sense of the miraculous', because it does not view language-games as *sacred*; but it is analogous 'in respect to the feeling of wonder and mystery'.

The obvious first point to make here is parallel to what I said above about explanation, namely that the *surroundings* of the wonder in the two cases are so very different as to make the force of any talk of an 'analogy' at best weak; even seriously vitiated by an apparent tendency to take 'the feeling of wonder and mystery' as a given, as something *common* to the two kinds of context he is comparing. I hesitate to ascribe such a thought to Malcolm, as it is an error of a kind against which he himself often vigorously argued. But the point is worth emphasizing on its own account. The nature of the 'feeling of wonder' is itself internally connected with the context in which it arises. I may wonder at the skill with which Boris Becker plays tennis. If I am asked what there is to wonder at I can, if I have the appropriate skill, explain the strategic thinking with which he plays and the difficulties involved in shots which he makes look easy, and so on. Compare that with this, written by Wittgenstein in 1947:

The miracles of nature.

One might say: art *shows* us the miracles of nature. It is based on the *concept* of the miracles of nature. (The blossom, just opening out. What is *marvellous* about it?) We say: 'Just look at it opening out!' [29]

Here there is no room for questions about what there is to wonder at; one must simply look. Perhaps one will see it, perhaps not; and here, 'seeing it' is hardly distinguishable from *reacting* to it in a certain way.

Wittgenstein made some further interesting remarks about the notion of the miraculous which are relevant here. For instance,

A miracle is, as it were, a *gesture* which God makes. As a man sits quietly and then makes an impressive gesture, God lets the world run on smoothly and then accompanies the words of a saint by a symbolic occurrence, a gesture of nature. It would be an instance if, when a saint has spoken, the trees around him bowed, as if in reverence. – Now, do I believe that this happens? I don't.

The only way for me to believe in a miracle in this sense would be to be *impressed* by an occurrence in this particular way. So that I should say e.g.: 'It was *impossible* to see these trees, and not to feel that they were responding to the words.' Just as I might say 'It is impossible to see the face of this dog and not to see that he is alert and full of attention to what his master is doing.' And I can imagine that the mere report of the *words* and life of a saint can make someone believe the reports that the trees bowed. But I am not so impressed. [30]

Suppose one asks what it means to be 'impressed in this particular way'. It is evident, I think, that the question can be answered only in the general kind of way Wittgenstein himself suggests, namely that it is finding oneself unable not to see the trees as bowing in reverence to the words of the saint. And one must not forget here the importance of the reference to the words *of a saint*. This invokes a concept which has its sense only in a context of religious belief.

In the present context it is also important to note Wittgenstein's comment that *he* is 'not so impressed'. To be clear about the conceptual question (what it means to speak of a 'miracle') is still a long, long way ('an infinite distance' Kierkegaard might have said) from actually seeing the situation in religious terms. More generally

Wittgenstein's philosophical insight into the limits of explanation, etc., even what one may rightly call his 'wonder' at what his investigations lay open to view, is an infinite distance from seeing the world, or human language-games, as the work of God. I do not believe that Wittgenstein would have taken such insight as a basis for saying he saw problems 'from a religious point of view'.

A sickness?

Malcolm's third 'analogy' is between the way Wittgenstein saw philosophical puzzles as symptoms of a 'disease of thinking' and such remarks as 'People are religious in the degree that they believe themselves to be not so much *imperfect* as *ill.*'

I do not want to say very much about this. Many of the remarks I made under the last two headings will, *mutatis mutandis*, apply here too. The senses in which one can speak of an 'illness' in each of these contexts is far too heavily dependent on the extremely diverse contexts involved for any talk of an analogy to carry much weight.

There is one more particular point I want to make. Malcolm emphasizes the *difficulty* Wittgenstein found in 'seeing what lay before his eyes' in the manner required for the healing of philosophical 'diseases' in himself; and he follows this by saying: 'He was convinced that religious commitment, at its deepest level, demands a complete turning round of one's life: but he surely felt that he could not, or would not, achieve that for himself.' With this last point Malcolm gets close to an important crux, closely connected with another point he makes that I have already alluded to, namely that religious believers often regard their faith itself as a *gift*. It seems to be implied by this way of thinking that what is here called 'religious commitment at its deepest level' is not something that *anyone* can achieve for him or herself, although of course one can discipline oneself in such a way as to perhaps make oneself receptive to faith. I think that there are already at this point signs of a *disanalogy*, rather than an analogy, with philosophy. While it makes sense to talk of a 'therapy' which would cure a person of the diseases of thinking that give rise to philosophy, one cannot speak in that way of the diseases of the soul which are the concern of religion. [31]

This has a connection with an interesting discussion in Chapter 1 of the following remark of Wittgenstein: 'I cannot kneel to pray because it's as though my knees are stiff. I am afraid of disintegration (of my disintegration), if I became too soft.' [32]

118

Taking up a suggestion of Roy Holland, Malcolm connects this with the intense commitment and concentration that Wittgenstein's philosophical work demanded of him: 'The "stiff knees" may be a metaphor for his stern posture of total engagement. Becoming soft would mean losing the tautness, the fighting alertness, that was required for him to pursue his ceaseless battles with the traps of language.'

There may well be truth in this. There is, however, a difficulty too that Malcolm's way of putting the matter brings to the fore. He says that Wittgenstein, in order to maintain his mental concentration, *resisted* an impulse he had to kneel in prayer. But the image of 'stiff knees' suggest something much less voluntaristic than this, something more like an internal obstacle that Wittgenstein encountered and which he was unable to overcome. In so far as we *do* think of what Wittgenstein was here saying in this way, it looks as though there would be not so much an *analogy* between a philosophical and a religious point of view, as Wittgenstein understood these, as a bitter *conflict*; as though the pursuit of philosophy would have *stood in the way* of his being able to see things from a religious point of view!

But the fairly sharp contrast I am here trying to draw between being unable, and being unwilling, to kneel in prayer has its own problems, brought out in the following passage:

Man's greatest happiness is love. Suppose you say of the schizophrenic: he does not love, he cannot love, he refuses to love – what is the difference?!

'He refuses to ...' means: it is in his power. And *who* wants to say that?

Well, what kind of thing do we say 'is in my power'? – We may say this when we want to draw a distinction. I can lift *this* weight, but I am not going to do it; I *cannot* lift that one.

'God has commanded it, therefore it must be possible to do it.' That means nothing. There is no 'therefore' about it. At most the two expressions might mean the *same*.

In this context 'He has commanded it' means roughly: 'He will punish anybody who doesn't do it.' And nothing follows from that about what anybody can or cannot do. And *that* is what 'predestination' means.[33]

The passage goes on to discuss further the concept of God's *punishments*, but the point I want to bring into focus here is the slipperiness in certain contexts of the difference between being *able* and being *willing* to do something. I think this difficulty certainly applies to the question of whether we should say that Wittgenstein was 'unwilling' or 'unable' to kneel in prayer.

I do not suggest that this discussion throws any direct light on Wittgenstein's conception of the relation between philosophy and religion. It does, however, raise interesting questions concerning the respective roles of intellect and will in both philosophy and religion. I shall not pursue these questions any further here.

Faith and works

The relation between intellect and will arises in a rather different way in Malcolm's fourth and last 'analogy'. He notes Wittgenstein's criticisms of the idea that faith needs to be, or could be, based on any intellectual 'proofs of God's existence' and connects this with the following:

> Wittgenstein would have agreed with St James that 'Faith, without works, is dead.' [His later works also emphasize] that our everyday concepts require a base of *acting, doing*, rather than reasoning or interpreting. ... 'it is our *acting*, which lies at the bottom of the language game'.

But although all these points are true enough, there is something misleading about juxtaposing them in this way.

First, the relation between faith and works, as this is understood by St James, is not simply a particular instance of the relation between thinking and acting, as this is discussed in, e.g., *Philosophical Investigations*. Faith, after all, has its expression in practices which St James is surely *distinguishing* from 'works': such as prayer, church attendance, religious observances and, in general, the language in which certain matters are discussed — a language which is in its turn used in connection with certain kinds of activity in ways about which members of the community of believers are in broad agreement. These too form 'a basis of human actions and reactions' which can give the concepts of religious belief a sort of sense. When Jesus criticized the Pharisees, he had in mind, and was, is, understood as having in mind, a certain characteristic way of acting and thinking, one which neglected the importance of 'works'. What matters in *this* context is the qualitative nature of the 'acting': namely, for instance, that it should be directed at the welfare of one's fellow human beings rather than *merely* at observance of religious forms.

Moreover, a faith which is expressed simply in religious observances without 'works' need have no connection with a desire for 'intellectual proofs'. A person may come to live in such a way for all sorts of reasons, as a result of upbringing, social pressure or ambition, even something that may be called 'religious conversion'. Conversely, a person who strives, in the context of a religious faith, to perform good works *may* at the same time attach much importance to 'intellectual proofs' in connection with it – whether or not we happen to think such a person confused.

As examples of ways in which faith needs expression in works Malcolm writes of 'helping others in concrete ways, treating their needs as equal to one's own, opening one's heart to them, not being cold or contemptuous, but loving'. Important as such acts and attitudes obviously are in connection with religious faith, their relation to it is by no means as straightforward as Malcolm's discussion may suggest. I have known at least one person, whose manner of life I would be prepared to describe in such a way, whom I would also say entirely lacked any religious sensibility and who indeed was one of those persons Malcolm describes at the beginning of Chapter 7, 'who take a serious view of religion, but regard it as a harmful influence, an obstacle to the fullest and best development of humanity'. More, very much more, needs to be said about precisely what it is that characterizes a love of humanity that is an expression of faith and what distinguishes it from one that is not. [34]

Something that Wittgenstein said to Drury, quoted by Malcolm in Chapter 1, is important here: 'It is my belief that only if you try to be helpful to other people will you in the end find your way to God.' It is important because Wittgenstein did *not* say that being helpful to other people *is* finding one's way to God, nor that it is a *sufficient condition* of doing so. He said it is a *necessary condition* of doing so. One cannot live a godly life *without* 'good works'; but all the same there is more to the godly life than that. And when Wittgenstein expressed regret, in a conversation with Drury, that he had been responsible for Drury's not having lived such a religious life as he might have done, I am sure he did not mean that he had been instrumental in preventing Drury from devoting his life to helping others.

There is a perhaps deeper philosophical point at issue here that I should like to try to bring into the open. Malcolm, particularly in the writings of his last years, rightly attached great importance to the role of what Wittgenstein called 'primitive reactions' in the formation of our concepts.[35] In his treatment of this issue Malcolm placed a great deal of emphasis on the *genetic* aspect of this role, i.e. that our more or less complicated language-games *grow out of* these much simpler primitive reactions. This led him to emphasize the *extra-linguistic* character of those reactions themselves. They are, or can be, reactions which are characteristic of human beings *before they ever learn to talk*.

Now there is a sense in which this is perfectly acceptable and is indeed an accurate *partial* representation of Wittgenstein's thinking. A famous case occurs in his discussion of the relation between pain and pain behaviour.

> How do words *refer* to sensations? – There doesn't seem to be any problem here; don't we talk about sensations every day, and give them names? But how is the connexion between the name and the thing named set up? This question is the same as: how does a human being learn the meaning of the names of sensations? – of the word 'pain' for example. Here is one possibility: words are connected with the primitive, the natural, expressions of the sensation and used in their place. A child has hurt himself and he cries; and then adults talk to him and teach him exclamations and, later, sentences. They teach the child new pain-behaviour.
>
> 'So you are saying that the word "pain" really means crying?' – On the contrary: the verbal expression of pain replaces crying and does not describe it.[36]

Another case occurs in his treatment of the concepts of cause and effect where he speaks of a primitive 'reaction towards a cause' , which is not the result of any thought, and suggests that we think of our sophisticated language-games with the word 'cause' as a development out of that.[37]

Let us look at this more closely. There are some points to notice about *Philosophical Investigations*, §244. First, the main point at issue in the discussion is *not*: how does our use of pain language develop?, but: what is it for words to *refer* to sensations? The developmental issue is raised for the light it throws on the latter question, because, perhaps, Wittgenstein suspects we have too simple-minded a preconception of how we learn to use words to refer: a preconception that is connected with, and feeds, a misunderstanding of what referring consists in. Second, if the genesis of our pain language were really the issue, Wittgenstein's discussion of it would look amazingly off-hand. 'Here is a possibility ...' is all he says. There is absolutely no attempt to verify whether his suggestion is correct as a matter of developmental psychology, absolutely no discussion of what other possibilities there might be and their relative merits. In fact it is clear, I think, that it is of no interest, as far as the issue Wittgenstein is discussing is concerned, whether his suggestion is right or not; it is *quite enough that the development could be thought of in that way*, since this in itself shows something all-important about what 'referring' *is* in this context. Third, the child's reactions, which form the basis of the teaching, are identified through the criteria of our existing language-game. Words are said to be substituted for the original, natural expression of *sensation*. The reaction is a reaction to *being hurt*. What the child is taught is new *pain behaviour*, i.e. this replaces an earlier form of *pain behaviour*. Of course, the italicized expressions here have their sense in the language-game a possible genesis of which Wittgenstein is suggesting.

Similar points apply, *mutatis mutandis*, to Wittgenstein's discussion of cause and effect. In this too he offers a suggestion about how we might come to *learn* the use of causal language as a way of bringing out a point about the *nature* of that language. His discussion here is particularly interesting because he explicitly warns *against* supposing that a historical development is what is at issue.

> The *basic form* of our game must be one in which there is no such thing as doubt. – What makes us sure of this? It can't surely be a matter of historical certainty.
>
> 'The basic form of the game can't include doubt.' What we are doing here above all is to *imagine* a basic form: a possibility, indeed a *very important* possibility. (We often confuse what is an important possibility with historical reality.) [38]

And here too the primitive reactions with which Wittgenstein compares our language-game are themselves described in terms taken from that language-game; they are seen from the point of view of that language-game. They are 'reactions *towards a cause*'. They have already been selected, according to criteria belonging to our developed language, from amongst the myriad ways in which a child acts and reacts.

I said earlier that in his treatment of Wittgenstein's talk about 'primitive reactions', Malcolm was led to emphasize the *extra-*

linguistic character of those reactions themselves. The above discussion is intended to bring out that there is a certain ambiguity in the meaning of 'extra-linguistic' here. It is perfectly true that we are speaking of reactions that people may have before they learn to talk; however, the language-games, a 'primitive form' of which we see in those reactions, provide the framework within which we identify in the first place the reactions of which we speak. Only thus are we able to make the distinctions between them which we need and which would be indiscernible, would indeed make no sense, if the wider context of the language-game were not presupposed.

I return now to the point from which I embarked on this digression: Malcolm's treatment of the relation between 'faith' and 'works' in Wittgenstein's thinking. I remarked that Malcolm seems sometimes to write as though we are dealing here with 'works' the nature of which can be understood independently of the ways in which they are or are not connected with a particular faith on the part of the doer, and I suggested that this is not so. I now want to suggest that the shortcoming which I see in Malcolm's treatment of this issue is closely connected with (is even perhaps another manifestation of) the error of emphasis I have claimed to find in his treatment of the relation between our 'primitive reactions' and our 'language-games'. He does not make sufficiently clear the internal connection that exists between the nature of the 'works' that are in question here and the use of the language of faith in the life of the believer.

'HOW CAN I BE A LOGICIAN BEFORE I AM A HUMAN BEING?'[39]

I remarked at the beginning of the present 'Discussion' that we do not *have* to think that, when Wittgenstein said he 'could not help seeing problems from a religious point of view', the *problems* he meant to include were *exclusively philosophical* problems. I argued that if we do not think Wittgenstein is to be so understood, the initial case for supposing that he might be speaking of some analogy between religious and philosophical problems is seriously damaged. I followed this with criticisms of the various analogies Malcolm suggests that Wittgenstein might have had in mind.

In this concluding section I want to consider in a very sketchy way an alternative point of view from which Wittgenstein's remark might perhaps be better understood. To make a start let us take as an example Wittgenstein's treatment of a problem which is not in itself exactly a philosophical problem but which may give us some insight into how Wittgenstein's remark might in fact be applied to his attitude to philosophical problems.

The problem is described by Drury at the end of 'Some notes on conversations with Wittgenstein'. [40] Drury had told Wittgenstein how distressed he was at his own ignorance and clumsiness in performing his medical duties during his first period of hospital residence as a newly trained doctor. Wittgenstein seemed at first to react in a somewhat off-hand way, saying simply that all Drury lacked was experience. But the next day Drury received the following (I think wonderful) letter from Wittgenstein:

Dear Drury,

I have thought a fair amount about our conversation on Sunday and I would like to say, or rather not to say but write, a few things about these conversations. Mainly I think this: Don't think about yourself, but think about others, e.g. your patients. You said in the Park yesterday that possibly you had made a mistake in taking up medicine: you immediately added that probably it was wrong to think such a thing at all. I am sure it is. But not because being a doctor you may not go the wrong way, or go to the dogs, but because if you do, this has nothing to do with your choice of profession being a mistake. For what human being can say what would have been the right thing if this is the wrong one? You didn't make a mistake because there was nothing at the time you knew or ought to have known that you overlooked. Only this one could have called making a mistake: and even if you had made a mistake in this sense, this would now have to be regarded as a datum as all the other circumstances inside and outside which you can't alter (control). The thing now is to live in the world in which you are, not to think or dream about the world you would like to be in. Look at people's sufferings, physical and mental, you have them close at hand, and this ought to be a good remedy for your troubles. Another way is to take a rest whenever you ought to take one and collect yourself. (Not with me because I wouldn't rest you.) As to religious thoughts I do not think the craving for placidity is religious: I think a religious person regards placidity or peace as a gift from heaven, not as something one ought to hunt after. Look at your patients more closely as human beings in trouble and enjoy more the opportunity you have to say 'good night' to so many people. This alone is a gift from heaven which many people would envy you. And this sort of thing ought to heal your frayed soul, I believe. It won't rest it; but when you are healthily tired you can just take a rest. I think in some sense you don't look at people's faces closely enough.

In conversations with me don't so much try to have the conversations which you think would taste well (though you will never get that anyway) but try to have the conversations which will have the pleasantest after-taste. It is most important that we should not one day have to tell ourselves that we had wasted the time we were allowed to spend together.

I wish you good thoughts but chiefly good feelings.

The letter as a whole seems to me a beautiful manifestation of what Wittgenstein was trying to say explicitly in the remark which is the subject of Malcolm's investigation, including the first part, 'I am not a religious man.' Where he speaks in explicitly religious terms he seems deliberately in a certain way to disclaim the authority to give religious advice. I am thinking of what he writes about 'religious thoughts' and 'placidity' : 'I do not think the craving for placidity is religious: I think a religious person regards placidity or peace as a gift from heaven, not as something one ought to hunt after.' He speaks, as it were, as an outsider in relation to religious faith. At the same time the letter as a whole is infused with religious sensibility: [41] the concern it expresses is clearly a sort of concern for Drury's *spiritual welfare*, one might say; and the language used at certain crucial points is poised on the edge of the religious. 'It is most important that we should not one day have to tell ourselves that we had wasted the time we were allowed to spend together.' The phrase 'allowed to spend together' would go very naturally with the conception of life as a gift, though its use does not in itself necessarily express a full commitment to the idea of life as a gift from God. It also clearly expresses the quasi-religious idea that life imposes certain duties on us (e.g. *not to waste* the opportunities offered us).

But for our present purposes the point of most interest is perhaps the way in which a major *philosophical* point is discussed in the context of this overall quasi-religious concern for Drury's spiritual health. I mean his treatment of the remark of Drury's that prompted the letter. In the first place he quite clearly treats Drury's fear that he had *made a mistake* in becoming a doctor as a philosophical confusion; and he brings out with the sort of characteristic pithiness familiar to us from his published philosophical writings the nature of that confusion. The following remarks could come straight out of a philosophical disquisition:

> You didn't make a mistake because there was nothing at the time you knew or ought to have known that you overlooked. Only this one could have called making a mistake: and even if you had made a mistake in this sense, this would now have to be regarded as a datum as all the other circumstances inside and outside which you can't alter (control).

In the present context however, the point clearly has overtones of a different sort. There are all sorts of ways in which someone might regard the consequences of a certain past decision 'as a datum'; but Wittgenstein connects the point clearly with a religious conception of *gratitude*. In fact the passage leads straight into a piece of spiritual advice which leans on the conception of the time one has in this life *as a gift*. Drury is enjoined to come to terms and accept the situation as it now is, namely that he *is* employed as a doctor; he is to realize that this brings with it certain peculiar opportunities, namely to be able to treat his sick patients genuinely as 'human beings in trouble' by properly 'looking at' them; and to have the opportunity 'to say "good night" to so many people'. It is precisely this that Wittgenstein identifies as a 'gift from heaven'.

There is a clear sense here of the importance – the spiritual importance, at least in certain circumstances – of philosophical clarity concerning the issue raised. Now of course, in writings intended *purely* for philosophical clarification the surroundings are different and we do not find Wittgenstein talking in the same way. We do not find him, for one thing, speaking so directly in the first person. But at the same time the 'passion' that is so clearly present in this letter still often makes itself heard.

I use the word 'passion' in this context in order deliberately to make a connection with certain remarks to be found in *Culture and Value* contrasting religion and 'wisdom':

> I believe that one of the things Christianity says is that sound doctrines are all useless. That you have to change your *life*. (Or the *direction* of your life.)

> It says that wisdom is all cold; and that you can no more use it for setting your life to rights than you can forge iron when it is *cold*.

The point is that a sound doctrine need not *take hold* of you; you can follow it as you would a doctor's prescription. – But here you need something to move you and turn you in a new direction. – (I.e. this is how I understand it.) Once you have been turned round, you must *stay* turned round.

Wisdom is passionless. But faith by contrast is what Kierkegaard calls a *passion*. [42]

Wisdom is cold and to that extent stupid. (Faith on the other hand is a passion.) It might also be said: Wisdom merely *conceals* life from you. Wisdom is like cold grey ash, covering up the glowing embers. [43]

Wittgenstein speaks in these passages of 'wisdom' rather than of 'philosophy' and I think it is clear that he cannot have meant here to contrast religion *directly* with philosophy. He had in mind rather, I should think, attempts to sum up the sense of a religion in philosophical or theological doctrines.

However, I think it is also clear that he would have been willing to say something in some ways analogous of the relation between religion and philosophy – that is to say, philosophy as he practised it. Certainly, as Malcolm brings out very well, he was passionately committed to philosophy and to a rare degree. But when he spoke of religion as a 'passion' through which one's life must be 'turned around' he was speaking of something different.

In 1944 he wrote the following:

No cry of torment can be greater than the cry of one man.

Or again, *no* torment can be greater than what a single human being may suffer.

A man is capable of infinite torment therefore, and so too he can stand in need of infinite help.

The Christian religion is only for the man who needs infinite help, solely, that is, for the man who experiences infinite torment.

The whole planet can suffer no greater torment than a *single* soul.

The Christian faith – as I see it – is a man's refuge in this *ultimate* torment.

Anyone in such torment who has the gift of opening his heart, rather than contracting it, accepts the means of salvation in his heart. [44]

He never spoke of philosophy in remotely similar terms. In fact, I think it is illuminating to put that last quotation alongside this: 'My idea is a certain coolness. A temple providing a setting for the passions without meddling with them.' [45] *Philosophical Investigations* it seems to me can be described in just this way. In it Wittgenstein's own voice, speaking in his own person, is rarely heard; he provides the context within which the various conflicting voices that together make up philosophical bewilderment can confront each other in a way that is otherwise usually impossible for them.

His own reference to Kierkegaard is extremely apposite in this connection. Kierkegaard's conception of philosophy was in many ways analogous to Wittgenstein's and his method of writing philosophy was in a parallel way designed to match this conception. Where, in Wittgenstein, the conflicting voices are brought together in a single conversation, in Kierkegaard they make themselves heard in separate, 'pseudonymous', works; but of course his work was intended to be read as a whole. Most important from our present point of view, perhaps, is the fact that Kierkegaard believed religious belief to stand at an 'infinite distance' from philosophical clarity. He did not believe that such clarity could by itself bring anyone one whit closer to religious faith.

I think that Wittgenstein would have taken the same view and this brings me back to my discussion of the letter to Drury. In what he writes about the philosophical confusion involved in Drury's talk of 'having made a mistake' in his choice of profession, I think there is a sense of the spiritual importance of philosophical clarity concerning the issue raised. He writes to someone he knows to be a religious person, drawing his attention to a confusion which he takes to be harmful to Drury's understanding of his own life, in a sense of 'harm' which itself is seen from Drury's religious perspective. There is of course no suggestion in this that a person who achieves philosophical clarity about such a point *ipso facto* will share such a perspective or be brought any closer to it.

At the same time I should like to say that, if we compare this passage with the kind of writing we find in Wittgenstein's strictly philosophical [46] works, we can sense in the latter too a spiritual dimension seldom met in the works of 'professional philosophers'. It is difficult to pin this down of course. It has partly to do with the passion to which Wittgenstein gives free rein in the dialogues between the various conflicting philosophical voices. This gives us a peculiar sense of the deep personal importance that the 'speakers' attach to the positions they defend. Typically, Wittgenstein tries to show that these speakers are confused, even deluded, in what they take this importance to consist in; his aim is to show us that what is really important is not to be found in this dimension at all. But I think we retain the sense that for someone to whom such philosophical issues matter [47] a lack of clarity about them can have grave implications for his or her own relation to life.

Here is an example. In his discussion of how such a sensation as pain can have a relation to a human *body*, we find the following:

> But isn't it absurd to say of a *body* that it has pain? – And why does one feel an absurdity in that? In what sense is it true that my hand does not feel pain, but I in my hand?
>
> What sort of issue is: Is it the *body* that feels pain? – How is it to be decided? What makes it plausible to say that it is *not* the body? – Well, something like this: If someone has a pain in his hand, then the hand does not say so (unless it writes it) and one does not comfort the hand, but the sufferer: one looks into his face. [48]

That last sentence gives me a wonderful sense of a fog suddenly lifting; the confused shapes that loom up and disappear again in the familiar philosophical discussions of 'mind and body' vanish and I am left with a clear view of something very familiar of which I had not noticed the importance. Its 'importance' lies in the first instance in its relation to the philosophical discussion. At the same time in attending to this minute detail that plays such an enormous role in our relations to each other, my sense of the dimensions of those relations is both transformed and enriched: when comforting someone who has been hurt, I look into the sufferer's eyes. Here is an illustration of what Wittgenstein may have meant in suggesting (in the passage I took as my epigraph) that the quoted verses from Longfellow could serve as his 'motto'. 'The gods' are there in 'each minute and unseen part'; and to make them apparent we must *pay attention* to those details. In Wittgenstein's letter to Drury precisely this detail is at the centre of his spiritual advice – 'I think in some sense you don't look at people's faces closely enough' – but that spiritual dimension is discernible clearly enough in *Philosophical Investigations* too.

I think one can see here something of what lay behind Wittgenstein's surprising remark to Russell: 'How can I be a logician before I am a human being?'; and also something of what lay behind the remark I quoted earlier from his Preface to *Philosophical Remarks:*

> I would like to say, 'this book is written to the glory of God', but nowadays this would be the trick of a cheat, i.e. it would not be correctly understood. It means the book was written in good will, and so far as it was not but was written from vanity etc., the author would wish to see it condemned. He can not make it more free of these impurities than he is himself.

Let me address myself to this second passage.

The last sentence: 'He can not make it more free of these impurities than he is himself', seems to me especially important in its implication that the 'purity' of the writer and the character of the writing are connected – and not just in a contingent way, but internally. It would not be easy to make such a claim with many, perhaps most, types of writing; but whether or not the point does have a more general application, I believe that for Wittgenstein philosophical writing was a special case. Here is one of his most explicit comments on this: 'Working in philosophy – like work in architecture in many respects – is really more a working on oneself. On one's own interpretation [*Auffassung*]. On one's way of seeing things. (And what one expects of them.)' [49] The comparison with architecture points us in the direction of a number of other remarks about architecture, which throw some light on the way in which Wittgenstein thought of the relation between the architect (philosopher) and his buildings (writings). Two of the most important for our present subject are:

> Remember the impression one gets from good architecture, that it expresses a thought. It makes one want to respond with a gesture. [50]

> Architecture is a *gesture*. Not every purposive movement of the human body is a gesture. And no more is every building designed for a purpose architecture. [51]

A gesture is *somebody's* gesture. If I find a gesture insulting, then I find the person who made it insulting (and if I am wrong about that I am wrong about the character of the gesture). Again if a gesture is vain or insincere then its maker is being vain or insincere in making it. We *do* of course read gestures in this way and such readings are both furthered by, and further, our understanding of the people who make them.

Wittgenstein's comparison between architecture and philosophy suggests we may say something similar about the relation between a piece of philosophical work [52] and its author. And clearly he himself invites us to do so in the quoted passage from the Preface to *Philosophical Remarks*. If we make this point the centre of our considerations, it will be clear that a comparison between religious and philosophical questions will not be the key to understanding what Wittgenstein meant by 'seeing problems from a religious point of view'.

Wittgenstein's conception of his life and of the problems with which it confronted him can certainly be called religious in the elusive but important sense spoken of earlier. His philosophical work was for him, moreover, one of the most important expressions of his life (the scene, as it were, of some of his most important 'gestures'). It is to be expected therefore that there should be a religious dimension to this work. The perspective I have tried to sketch in this last section offers a much less clear-cut interpretation than do Malcolm's 'analogies' of what he meant in the remark to Drury to the discussion of which this book has been devoted; but my own view is that we should not expect a very clear-cut account of what Wittgenstein meant. I am grateful to Norman Malcolm, as for so much else, for making me think about the whole issue in a way I should probably not otherwise have come to. Of course he himself explicitly disclaimed any pretensions to finality or certainty in his interpretation. And I want to make the same sort of disclaimer.

NOTES

I am grateful to Helen Geyer for her many perceptive comments, which resulted in substantial improvements.

1 Ludwig Wittgenstein, *Culture and Value*, ed. G. H. von Wright and H. Nyman, tr. Peter Winch, Oxford, Blackwell, 1980, p. 34[e]. *Culture and Value* is published with the German and English versions *en face*. The superscript 'e' refers to the English translation.

2 I am thinking here of Wittgenstein's 'confessions', referred to in various places in Rush Rhees (ed.), *Ludwig Wittgenstein, Personal Recollections*, Oxford, Oxford University Press, 1984, and discussed very illuminatingly by Rhees himself in his Postscript to that volume.

3 See Brian McGuinness, *Wittgenstein: A Life: Young Ludwig (1889–1921)*, London, Duckworth, 1988, chapter 7: 'The War 1914–18'.

4 On the notion of living 'decently' (*anständig*) as Wittgenstein understood it see Rush Rhees's Postscript to his *Ludwig Wittgenstein, Personal Recollections*.

5 Rhees, *Wittgenstein*, p. 93.

6 cf. *Culture and Value*, p. 25^e.

7 Here it is of course particularly important to observe the distinction between Wittgenstein's own religious reflections and his philosophical comments on religious discourse.

8 See also his *Memory and Mind*, Ithaca, Cornell University Press, 1977 and *Nothing is Hidden*, Oxford, Blackwell, 1986.

9 See for instance his letter to Moritz Schlick of 8 August 1932: 'ich kann mir nicht denken, daß Carnap die letzten Sätze der "Abhandlung" – und also den Grundgedanken des ganzen Buches – so ganz und gar mißverstanden haben sollte.' *Ludwig Wittgenstein, Sein Leben in Bildern und Texten*, ed. M. Nedo and M. Ranchetti, Frankfurt am Main, Suhrkamp, 1983, p. 255. (' … and I cannot imagine that Carnap should have so completely misunderstood the last sentences of the *Tractatus* – and hence the fundamental idea of the whole book.')

10 'Throwing away the top of the ladder', *Yale Review*, vol. 79, no. 3:

11 I shall leave on one side here the reasons for which Wittgenstein later came to think he had failed in this attempt. See my paper, 'Persuasion', *Midwest Studies in Philosophy*, vol. 17, 1992. Earlier, in the chapter 'Language, thought and world in Wittgenstein's *Tractatus*' (Peter Winch, *Trying to Make Sense*, Oxford, Blackwell, 1987, chapter 2) I tried to show, against Malcolm, how the apparently metaphysical propositions of the earlier part of the *Tractatus* must, in the light of the subsequent discussion, be read as misbegotten attempts to state logico-syntactical points which can, properly speaking, only be 'shown'. I did not succeed in convincing Norman. His characteristic comment on a draft of the chapter in question was: 'Your paper is very persuasive, Peter. The only trouble is, it doesn't persuade me.'

12 The alternative – and in my view correct – reading is that Wittgenstein is here referring to the relation between the usual linguistic form in which propositions are expressed and the way – only revealed by 'logical analysis' – in which such propositions are constructed through truth-functional operations out of 'elementary propositions'.

13 'The method of projection is the thinking of the sense of the proposition.'

14 3.12 Die Projektionsmethode ist die Art und Weise der Anwendung des Satzzeichens. 3.13 Die Anwendung des Satzzeichens ist das Denken seines Sinnes (L. Wittgenstein, *Logisch-philosophische Abhandlung/Tractatus Logico-Philosophicus*, Kritische edition, ed. Brian McGuinness and Joachim Schulte, Frankfurt am Main, Suhrkamp, 1989, p. 19). The preceding discussion of this issue is an adaption of an earlier treatment. See pp. 13–14 of my *Trying to Make Sense*.

15 I have tried to assess the importance of this in 'Persuasion'.

16 Ludwig Wittgenstein, *On Certainty*, ed. G. E. M. Anscombe and G. H. von Wright, tr. D. Paul and G. E. M. Anscombe, Oxford, Blackwell, 1969, §191.

17 Norman Malcolm, *Memory and Mind*, Ithaca, Cornell University Press, 1977.

18 Perhaps this should read: 'The ways people have had ...'.

19 Rush Rhees, *Ludwig Wittgenstein, Personal Recollections*, p. 108.

20 William James, *Varieties of Religious Experience*, London, Longmans, 1952.

21 For instance in *Lectures and Conversations on Aesthetics, Psychology and Religious Belief*, ed. Cyril Barrett, Oxford, Blackwell, 1966.

22 *Culture and Value*, p. 85^e.

23 *Culture and Value*, p. 71^e. Wittgenstein seems to take the phrase 'the cussedness of things', which is how I have translated 'die Tücke des Objekts', as offering an explanation of some particular misfortune by reference to a malignancy present in the particular situation. On my own understanding 'the cussedness of things' rather expresses a general attitude to the constitution of the world rather like that which Wittgenstein goes on to describe as an alternative and better way of looking at things. Native German speakers tell me that they would also understand 'Die Tücke des Objekts' in this way. None of this of course makes any difference to the point Wittgenstein is making.

24 *Culture and Value*, p. 85^e.

25 On this topic see for instance 'Religion and language' in Rush Rhees, *Without Answers*, London, Routledge & Kegan Paul, 1969.

26 *Culture and Value*, p. 11^e.

27 *Culture and Value*, p. 57^e.

28 'A lecture on ethics', *Philosophical Review*, vol. 74, no. 1, January 1965.

29 *Culture and Value*, p. 56^e.

30 *Culture and Value*, p. 45^e.

31 This is no doubt connected with the differences Kierkegaard discusses between the religious and the philosophical 'teacher'.

32 *Culture and Value*, p. 56^e.

33 *Culture and Value*, p. 77^e.

34 Rush Rhees's 'Religion and language', in his *Without Answers*, is extremely pertinent here.

35 See especially his article 'Wittgenstein: the relation of language to instinctive behaviour', *Philosophical Investigations*, vol. 5, no. 1, 1981.

36 *Philosophical Investigations*, 244.

37 Ludwig Wittgenstein, 'Cause and effect: intuitive awareness', ed. Rush Rhees, tr. Peter Winch, *Philosophia*, vol. 6, nos 3 and 4, 1976.

38 *Philosophia*, p. 411.

39 The quotation is from a letter (translated by B. F. McGuinness) quoted by Rush Rhees in *Ludwig Wittgenstein, Personal Recollections*. p. 211. The full text quoted by Rhees is as follows:

Und ich hoffe immer noch es werde endlich einmal ein endgültiger Ausbruch erfolgen, und ich kann ein anderer Mensch werden. . . . Vielleicht glaubst Du, daß es Zeitverschwendung ist, über mich selbst zu denken; aber wie kann ich Logiker sein, wenn ich noch nicht Mensch bin! *Vor allem* muß ich mit mir selbst in's Reine kommen!

40 Rhees, *Ludwig Wittgenstein, Personal Recollections*, pp. 109–10.
41 At this point I refer back to my remarks on pp. 108-10 about the difficulties in speaking in this way.
42 *Culture and Value*, p. 53^e.
43 *Culture and Value*, p. 56^e.
44 *Culture and Value*, p. 46^e.
45 *Culture and Value*, p. 2^e.
46 Here I feel the lack of any word in English that carries quite the sense of the German '*wissenschaftlich*'! The obvious translation, 'scientific', would be very misleading because this is much more closely associated with natural science than is the German; and, more particularly, because of the care Wittgenstein took to distinguish philosophical from scientific questions.
47 I make this qualification since I am sure that Wittgenstein did *not* – like Socrates? – want to make philosophical clarity quite generally a *sine qua non* of spiritual health.
48 *Philosophical Investigations*, §286.
49 *Culture and Value*, p. 16^e. The comparison with architecture is no doubt due in large part to Wittgenstein's own experience in building the house for his sister, Margarethe, though architecture is a peculiarly apposite case to which to apply the term 'a gesture'. But there is no reason not to think that, given the right context, something similar could be said of other human productions. In fact Wittgenstein sometimes writes of music in a similar vein.
50 *Culture and Value*, p. 22^e.
51 *Culture and Value*, p. 42^e.
52 That is, a piece of philosophical work that makes the same kind of claim on our attention as does Wittgenstein's.

INDEX